C-4   CAREER EXAMINATION SERIES

This is your
PASSBOOK for...

Accountant-Auditor

Test Preparation Study Guide
Questions & Answers

NATIONAL LEARNING CORPORATION®

COPYRIGHT NOTICE

This book is SOLELY intended for, is sold ONLY to, and its use is RESTRICTED to individual, bona fide applicants or candidates who qualify by virtue of having seriously filed applications for appropriate license, certificate, professional and/or promotional advancement, higher school matriculation, scholarship, or other legitimate requirements of education and/or governmental authorities.

This book is NOT intended for use, class instruction, tutoring, training, duplication, copying, reprinting, excerption, or adaptation, etc., by:

1) Other publishers
2) Proprietors and/or Instructors of "Coaching" and/or Preparatory Courses
3) Personnel and/or Training Divisions of commercial, industrial, and governmental organizations
4) Schools, colleges, or universities and/or their departments and staffs, including teachers and other personnel
5) Testing Agencies or Bureaus
6) Study groups which seek by the purchase of a single volume to copy and/or duplicate and/or adapt this material for use by the group as a whole without having purchased individual volumes for each of the members of the group
7) Et al.

Such persons would be in violation of appropriate Federal and State statutes.

PROVISION OF LICENSING AGREEMENTS – Recognized educational, commercial, industrial, and governmental institutions and organizations, and others legitimately engaged in educational pursuits, including training, testing, and measurement activities, may address request for a licensing agreement to the copyright owners, who will determine whether, and under what conditions, including fees and charges, the materials in this book may be used them. In other words, a licensing facility exists for the legitimate use of the material in this book on other than an individual basis. However, it is asseverated and affirmed here that the material in this book CANNOT be used without the receipt of the express permission of such a licensing agreement from the Publishers. Inquiries re licensing should be addressed to the company, attention rights and permissions department.

All rights reserved, including the right of reproduction in whole or in part, in any form or by any means, electronic or mechanical, including photocopying, recording, or by any information storage and retrieval system, without permission in writing from the Publisher.

Copyright © 2024 by
National Learning Corporation

212 Michael Drive, Syosset, NY 11791
(516) 921-8888 • www.passbooks.com
E-mail: info@passbooks.com

PASSBOOK® SERIES

THE *PASSBOOK® SERIES* has been created to prepare applicants and candidates for the ultimate academic battlefield – the examination room.

At some time in our lives, each and every one of us may be required to take an examination – for validation, matriculation, admission, qualification, registration, certification, or licensure.

Based on the assumption that every applicant or candidate has met the basic formal educational standards, has taken the required number of courses, and read the necessary texts, the *PASSBOOK® SERIES* furnishes the one special preparation which may assure passing with confidence, instead of failing with insecurity. Examination questions – together with answers – are furnished as the basic vehicle for study so that the mysteries of the examination and its compounding difficulties may be eliminated or diminished by a sure method.

This book is meant to help you pass your examination provided that you qualify and are serious in your objective.

The entire field is reviewed through the huge store of content information which is succinctly presented through a provocative and challenging approach – the question-and-answer method.

A climate of success is established by furnishing the correct answers at the end of each test.

You soon learn to recognize types of questions, forms of questions, and patterns of questioning. You may even begin to anticipate expected outcomes.

You perceive that many questions are repeated or adapted so that you can gain acute insights, which may enable you to score many sure points.

You learn how to confront new questions, or types of questions, and to attack them confidently and work out the correct answers.

You note objectives and emphases, and recognize pitfalls and dangers, so that you may make positive educational adjustments.

Moreover, you are kept fully informed in relation to new concepts, methods, practices, and directions in the field.

You discover that you are actually taking the examination all the time: you are preparing for the examination by "taking" an examination, not by reading extraneous and/or supererogatory textbooks.

In short, this PASSBOOK®, used directedly, should be an important factor in helping you to pass your test.

ACCOUNTANT-AUDITOR

DUTIES
Perform professional accounting and auditing duties in the development, examination, review, audit, or analysis of accounting records and systems and may be given supervisory responsibility for the operation of a moderately complex accounting system. They may also perform field audits of governmental, quasi-governmental and/or private organizations to assure that accounts and other records are in compliance with all pertinent law, rules, regulations and procedures.

SUBJECT OF EXAMINATION
The multiple-choice written test will cover knowledge, skills, and/or abilities in such areas as:
1. General accounting;
2. General auditing;
3. Understanding and interpreting written material;
4. Interpreting tabular material; and
5. Preparing written material.

HOW TO TAKE A TEST

I. YOU MUST PASS AN EXAMINATION

A. WHAT EVERY CANDIDATE SHOULD KNOW

Examination applicants often ask us for help in preparing for the written test. What can I study in advance? What kinds of questions will be asked? How will the test be given? How will the papers be graded?

As an applicant for a civil service examination, you may be wondering about some of these things. Our purpose here is to suggest effective methods of advance study and to describe civil service examinations.

Your chances for success on this examination can be increased if you know how to prepare. Those "pre-examination jitters" can be reduced if you know what to expect. You can even experience an adventure in good citizenship if you know why civil service exams are given.

B. WHY ARE CIVIL SERVICE EXAMINATIONS GIVEN?

Civil service examinations are important to you in two ways. As a citizen, you want public jobs filled by employees who know how to do their work. As a job seeker, you want a fair chance to compete for that job on an equal footing with other candidates. The best-known means of accomplishing this two-fold goal is the competitive examination.

Exams are widely publicized throughout the nation. They may be administered for jobs in federal, state, city, municipal, town or village governments or agencies.

Any citizen may apply, with some limitations, such as the age or residence of applicants. Your experience and education may be reviewed to see whether you meet the requirements for the particular examination. When these requirements exist, they are reasonable and applied consistently to all applicants. Thus, a competitive examination may cause you some uneasiness now, but it is your privilege and safeguard.

C. HOW ARE CIVIL SERVICE EXAMS DEVELOPED?

Examinations are carefully written by trained technicians who are specialists in the field known as "psychological measurement," in consultation with recognized authorities in the field of work that the test will cover. These experts recommend the subject matter areas or skills to be tested; only those knowledges or skills important to your success on the job are included. The most reliable books and source materials available are used as references. Together, the experts and technicians judge the difficulty level of the questions.

Test technicians know how to phrase questions so that the problem is clearly stated. Their ethics do not permit "trick" or "catch" questions. Questions may have been tried out on sample groups, or subjected to statistical analysis, to determine their usefulness.

Written tests are often used in combination with performance tests, ratings of training and experience, and oral interviews. All of these measures combine to form the best-known means of finding the right person for the right job.

II. HOW TO PASS THE WRITTEN TEST

A. NATURE OF THE EXAMINATION

To prepare intelligently for civil service examinations, you should know how they differ from school examinations you have taken. In school you were assigned certain definite pages to read or subjects to cover. The examination questions were quite detailed and usually emphasized memory. Civil service exams, on the other hand, try to discover your present ability to perform the duties of a position, plus your potentiality to learn these duties. In other words, a civil service exam attempts to predict how successful you will be. Questions cover such a broad area that they cannot be as minute and detailed as school exam questions.

In the public service similar kinds of work, or positions, are grouped together in one "class." This process is known as *position-classification*. All the positions in a class are paid according to the salary range for that class. One class title covers all of these positions, and they are all tested by the same examination.

B. FOUR BASIC STEPS

1) Study the announcement

How, then, can you know what subjects to study? Our best answer is: "Learn as much as possible about the class of positions for which you've applied." The exam will test the knowledge, skills and abilities needed to do the work.

Your most valuable source of information about the position you want is the official exam announcement. This announcement lists the training and experience qualifications. Check these standards and apply only if you come reasonably close to meeting them.

The brief description of the position in the examination announcement offers some clues to the subjects which will be tested. Think about the job itself. Review the duties in your mind. Can you perform them, or are there some in which you are rusty? Fill in the blank spots in your preparation.

Many jurisdictions preview the written test in the exam announcement by including a section called "Knowledge and Abilities Required," "Scope of the Examination," or some similar heading. Here you will find out specifically what fields will be tested.

2) Review your own background

Once you learn in general what the position is all about, and what you need to know to do the work, ask yourself which subjects you already know fairly well and which need improvement. You may wonder whether to concentrate on improving your strong areas or on building some background in your fields of weakness. When the announcement has specified "some knowledge" or "considerable knowledge," or has used adjectives like "beginning principles of..." or "advanced ... methods," you can get a clue as to the number and difficulty of questions to be asked in any given field. More questions, and hence broader coverage, would be included for those subjects which are more important in the work. Now weigh your strengths and weaknesses against the job requirements and prepare accordingly.

3) Determine the level of the position

Another way to tell how intensively you should prepare is to understand the level of the job for which you are applying. Is it the entering level? In other words, is this the position in which beginners in a field of work are hired? Or is it an intermediate or advanced level? Sometimes this is indicated by such words as "Junior" or "Senior" in the class title. Other jurisdictions use Roman numerals to designate the level – Clerk I, Clerk II, for example. The word "Supervisor" sometimes appears in the title. If the level is not indicated by the title, check the description of duties. Will you be working under very close supervision, or will you have responsibility for independent decisions in this work?

4) Choose appropriate study materials

Now that you know the subjects to be examined and the relative amount of each subject to be covered, you can choose suitable study materials. For beginning level jobs, or even advanced ones, if you have a pronounced weakness in some aspect of your training, read a modern, standard textbook in that field. Be sure it is up to date and has general coverage. Such books are normally available at your library, and the librarian will be glad to help you locate one. For entry-level positions, questions of appropriate difficulty are chosen -- neither highly advanced questions, nor those too simple. Such questions require careful thought but not advanced training.

If the position for which you are applying is technical or advanced, you will read more advanced, specialized material. If you are already familiar with the basic principles of your field, elementary textbooks would waste your time. Concentrate on advanced textbooks and technical periodicals. Think through the concepts and review difficult problems in your field.

These are all general sources. You can get more ideas on your own initiative, following these leads. For example, training manuals and publications of the government agency which employs workers in your field can be useful, particularly for technical and professional positions. A letter or visit to the government department involved may result in more specific study suggestions, and certainly will provide you with a more definite idea of the exact nature of the position you are seeking.

III. KINDS OF TESTS

Tests are used for purposes other than measuring knowledge and ability to perform specified duties. For some positions, it is equally important to test ability to make adjustments to new situations or to profit from training. In others, basic mental abilities not dependent on information are essential. Questions which test these things may not appear as pertinent to the duties of the position as those which test for knowledge and information. Yet they are often highly important parts of a fair examination. For very general questions, it is almost impossible to help you direct your study efforts. What we can do is to point out some of the more common of these general abilities needed in public service positions and describe some typical questions.

1) General information

Broad, general information has been found useful for predicting job success in some kinds of work. This is tested in a variety of ways, from vocabulary lists to questions about current events. Basic background in some field of work, such as sociology or economics, may be sampled in a group of questions. Often these are principles which have become familiar to most persons through exposure rather than through formal training. It is difficult to advise you how to study for these questions; being alert to the world around you is our best suggestion.

2) Verbal ability

An example of an ability needed in many positions is verbal or language ability. Verbal ability is, in brief, the ability to use and understand words. Vocabulary and grammar tests are typical measures of this ability. Reading comprehension or paragraph interpretation questions are common in many kinds of civil service tests. You are given a paragraph of written material and asked to find its central meaning.

3) Numerical ability

Number skills can be tested by the familiar arithmetic problem, by checking paired lists of numbers to see which are alike and which are different, or by interpreting charts and graphs. In the latter test, a graph may be printed in the test booklet which you are asked to use as the basis for answering questions.

4) Observation

A popular test for law-enforcement positions is the observation test. A picture is shown to you for several minutes, then taken away. Questions about the picture test your ability to observe both details and larger elements.

5) Following directions

In many positions in the public service, the employee must be able to carry out written instructions dependably and accurately. You may be given a chart with several columns, each column listing a variety of information. The questions require you to carry out directions involving the information given in the chart.

6) Skills and aptitudes

Performance tests effectively measure some manual skills and aptitudes. When the skill is one in which you are trained, such as typing or shorthand, you can practice. These tests are often very much like those given in business school or high school courses. For many of the other skills and aptitudes, however, no short-time preparation can be made. Skills and abilities natural to you or that you have developed throughout your lifetime are being tested.

Many of the general questions just described provide all the data needed to answer the questions and ask you to use your reasoning ability to find the answers. Your best preparation for these tests, as well as for tests of facts and ideas, is to be at your physical and mental best. You, no doubt, have your own methods of getting into an exam-taking mood and keeping "in shape." The next section lists some ideas on this subject.

IV. KINDS OF QUESTIONS

Only rarely is the "essay" question, which you answer in narrative form, used in civil service tests. Civil service tests are usually of the short-answer type. Full instructions for answering these questions will be given to you at the examination. But in case this is your first experience with short-answer questions and separate answer sheets, here is what you need to know:

1) **Multiple-choice Questions**

Most popular of the short-answer questions is the "multiple choice" or "best answer" question. It can be used, for example, to test for factual knowledge, ability to solve problems or judgment in meeting situations found at work.

A multiple-choice question is normally one of three types—
- It can begin with an incomplete statement followed by several possible endings. You are to find the one ending which *best* completes the statement, although some of the others may not be entirely wrong.
- It can also be a complete statement in the form of a question which is answered by choosing one of the statements listed.

- It can be in the form of a problem – again you select the best answer.

Here is an example of a multiple-choice question with a discussion which should give you some clues as to the method for choosing the right answer:

When an employee has a complaint about his assignment, the action which will *best* help him overcome his difficulty is to
- A. discuss his difficulty with his coworkers
- B. take the problem to the head of the organization
- C. take the problem to the person who gave him the assignment
- D. say nothing to anyone about his complaint

In answering this question, you should study each of the choices to find which is best. Consider choice "A" – Certainly an employee may discuss his complaint with fellow employees, but no change or improvement can result, and the complaint remains unresolved. Choice "B" is a poor choice since the head of the organization probably does not know what assignment you have been given, and taking your problem to him is known as "going over the head" of the supervisor. The supervisor, or person who made the assignment, is the person who can clarify it or correct any injustice. Choice "C" is, therefore, correct. To say nothing, as in choice "D," is unwise. Supervisors have and interest in knowing the problems employees are facing, and the employee is seeking a solution to his problem.

2) True/False Questions

The "true/false" or "right/wrong" form of question is sometimes used. Here a complete statement is given. Your job is to decide whether the statement is right or wrong.

SAMPLE: A roaming cell-phone call to a nearby city costs less than a non-roaming call to a distant city.

This statement is wrong, or false, since roaming calls are more expensive.

This is not a complete list of all possible question forms, although most of the others are variations of these common types. You will always get complete directions for answering questions. Be sure you understand *how* to mark your answers – ask questions until you do.

V. RECORDING YOUR ANSWERS

Computer terminals are used more and more today for many different kinds of exams.
For an examination with very few applicants, you may be told to record your answers in the test booklet itself. Separate answer sheets are much more common. If this separate answer sheet is to be scored by machine – and this is often the case – it is highly important that you mark your answers correctly in order to get credit.
An electronic scoring machine is often used in civil service offices because of the speed with which papers can be scored. Machine-scored answer sheets must be marked with a pencil, which will be given to you. This pencil has a high graphite content which responds to the electronic scoring machine. As a matter of fact, stray dots may register as answers, so do not let your pencil rest on the answer sheet while you are pondering the correct answer. Also, if your pencil lead breaks or is otherwise defective, ask for another.

Since the answer sheet will be dropped in a slot in the scoring machine, be careful not to bend the corners or get the paper crumpled.

The answer sheet normally has five vertical columns of numbers, with 30 numbers to a column. These numbers correspond to the question numbers in your test booklet. After each number, going across the page are four or five pairs of dotted lines. These short dotted lines have small letters or numbers above them. The first two pairs may also have a "T" or "F" above the letters. This indicates that the first two pairs only are to be used if the questions are of the true-false type. If the questions are multiple choice, disregard the "T" and "F" and pay attention only to the small letters or numbers.

Answer your questions in the manner of the sample that follows:

32. The largest city in the United States is
    A. Washington, D.C.
    B. New York City
    C. Chicago
    D. Detroit
    E. San Francisco

1) Choose the answer you think is best. (New York City is the largest, so "B" is correct.)
2) Find the row of dotted lines numbered the same as the question you are answering. (Find row number 32)
3) Find the pair of dotted lines corresponding to the answer. (Find the pair of lines under the mark "B.")
4) Make a solid black mark between the dotted lines.

VI. BEFORE THE TEST

Common sense will help you find procedures to follow to get ready for an examination. Too many of us, however, overlook these sensible measures. Indeed, nervousness and fatigue have been found to be the most serious reasons why applicants fail to do their best on civil service tests. Here is a list of reminders:

- Begin your preparation early – Don't wait until the last minute to go scurrying around for books and materials or to find out what the position is all about.
- Prepare continuously – An hour a night for a week is better than an all-night cram session. This has been definitely established. What is more, a night a week for a month will return better dividends than crowding your study into a shorter period of time.
- Locate the place of the exam – You have been sent a notice telling you when and where to report for the examination. If the location is in a different town or otherwise unfamiliar to you, it would be well to inquire the best route and learn something about the building.
- Relax the night before the test – Allow your mind to rest. Do not study at all that night. Plan some mild recreation or diversion; then go to bed early and get a good night's sleep.
- Get up early enough to make a leisurely trip to the place for the test – This way unforeseen events, traffic snarls, unfamiliar buildings, etc. will not upset you.
- Dress comfortably – A written test is not a fashion show. You will be known by number and not by name, so wear something comfortable.

- Leave excess paraphernalia at home – Shopping bags and odd bundles will get in your way. You need bring only the items mentioned in the official notice you received; usually everything you need is provided. Do not bring reference books to the exam. They will only confuse those last minutes and be taken away from you when in the test room.
- Arrive somewhat ahead of time – If because of transportation schedules you must get there very early, bring a newspaper or magazine to take your mind off yourself while waiting.
- Locate the examination room – When you have found the proper room, you will be directed to the seat or part of the room where you will sit. Sometimes you are given a sheet of instructions to read while you are waiting. Do not fill out any forms until you are told to do so; just read them and be prepared.
- Relax and prepare to listen to the instructions
- If you have any physical problem that may keep you from doing your best, be sure to tell the test administrator. If you are sick or in poor health, you really cannot do your best on the exam. You can come back and take the test some other time.

VII. AT THE TEST

The day of the test is here and you have the test booklet in your hand. The temptation to get going is very strong. Caution! There is more to success than knowing the right answers. You must know how to identify your papers and understand variations in the type of short-answer question used in this particular examination. Follow these suggestions for maximum results from your efforts:

1) Cooperate with the monitor

The test administrator has a duty to create a situation in which you can be as much at ease as possible. He will give instructions, tell you when to begin, check to see that you are marking your answer sheet correctly, and so on. He is not there to guard you, although he will see that your competitors do not take unfair advantage. He wants to help you do your best.

2) Listen to all instructions

Don't jump the gun! Wait until you understand all directions. In most civil service tests you get more time than you need to answer the questions. So don't be in a hurry. Read each word of instructions until you clearly understand the meaning. Study the examples, listen to all announcements and follow directions. Ask questions if you do not understand what to do.

3) Identify your papers

Civil service exams are usually identified by number only. You will be assigned a number; you must not put your name on your test papers. Be sure to copy your number correctly. Since more than one exam may be given, copy your exact examination title.

4) Plan your time

Unless you are told that a test is a "speed" or "rate of work" test, speed itself is usually not important. Time enough to answer all the questions will be provided, but this does not mean that you have all day. An overall time limit has been set. Divide the total time (in minutes) by the number of questions to determine the approximate time you have for each question.

5) Do not linger over difficult questions

If you come across a difficult question, mark it with a paper clip (useful to have along) and come back to it when you have been through the booklet. One caution if you do this – be sure to skip a number on your answer sheet as well. Check often to be sure that you have not lost your place and that you are marking in the row numbered the same as the question you are answering.

6) Read the questions

Be sure you know what the question asks! Many capable people are unsuccessful because they failed to *read* the questions correctly.

7) Answer all questions

Unless you have been instructed that a penalty will be deducted for incorrect answers, it is better to guess than to omit a question.

8) Speed tests

It is often better NOT to guess on speed tests. It has been found that on timed tests people are tempted to spend the last few seconds before time is called in marking answers at random – without even reading them – in the hope of picking up a few extra points. To discourage this practice, the instructions may warn you that your score will be "corrected" for guessing. That is, a penalty will be applied. The incorrect answers will be deducted from the correct ones, or some other penalty formula will be used.

9) Review your answers

If you finish before time is called, go back to the questions you guessed or omitted to give them further thought. Review other answers if you have time.

10) Return your test materials

If you are ready to leave before others have finished or time is called, take ALL your materials to the monitor and leave quietly. Never take any test material with you. The monitor can discover whose papers are not complete, and taking a test booklet may be grounds for disqualification.

VIII. EXAMINATION TECHNIQUES

1) Read the general instructions carefully. These are usually printed on the first page of the exam booklet. As a rule, these instructions refer to the timing of the examination; the fact that you should not start work until the signal and must stop work at a signal, etc. If there are any *special* instructions, such as a choice of questions to be answered, make sure that you note this instruction carefully.

2) When you are ready to start work on the examination, that is as soon as the signal has been given, read the instructions to each question booklet, underline any key words or phrases, such as *least, best, outline, describe* and the like. In this way you will tend to answer as requested rather than discover on reviewing your paper that you *listed without describing*, that you selected the *worst* choice rather than the *best* choice, etc.

3) If the examination is of the objective or multiple-choice type – that is, each question will also give a series of possible answers: A, B, C or D, and you are called upon to select the best answer and write the letter next to that answer on your answer paper – it is advisable to start answering each question in turn. There may be anywhere from 50 to 100 such questions in the three or four hours allotted and you can see how much time would be taken if you read through all the questions before beginning to answer any. Furthermore, if you come across a question or group of questions which you know would be difficult to answer, it would undoubtedly affect your handling of all the other questions.

4) If the examination is of the essay type and contains but a few questions, it is a moot point as to whether you should read all the questions before starting to answer any one. Of course, if you are given a choice – say five out of seven and the like – then it is essential to read all the questions so you can eliminate the two that are most difficult. If, however, you are asked to answer all the questions, there may be danger in trying to answer the easiest one first because you may find that you will spend too much time on it. The best technique is to answer the first question, then proceed to the second, etc.

5) Time your answers. Before the exam begins, write down the time it started, then add the time allowed for the examination and write down the time it must be completed, then divide the time available somewhat as follows:
   - If 3-1/2 hours are allowed, that would be 210 minutes. If you have 80 objective-type questions, that would be an average of 2-1/2 minutes per question. Allow yourself no more than 2 minutes per question, or a total of 160 minutes, which will permit about 50 minutes to review.
   - If for the time allotment of 210 minutes there are 7 essay questions to answer, that would average about 30 minutes a question. Give yourself only 25 minutes per question so that you have about 35 minutes to review.

6) The most important instruction is to *read each question* and make sure you know what is wanted. The second most important instruction is to *time yourself properly* so that you answer every question. The third most important instruction is to *answer every question*. Guess if you have to but include something for each question. Remember that you will receive no credit for a blank and will probably receive some credit if you write something in answer to an essay question. If you guess a letter – say "B" for a multiple-choice question – you may have guessed right. If you leave a blank as an answer to a multiple-choice question, the examiners may respect your feelings but it will not add a point to your score. Some exams may penalize you for wrong answers, so in such cases *only*, you may not want to guess unless you have some basis for your answer.

7) Suggestions
   a. Objective-type questions
      1. Examine the question booklet for proper sequence of pages and questions
      2. Read all instructions carefully
      3. Skip any question which seems too difficult; return to it after all other questions have been answered
      4. Apportion your time properly; do not spend too much time on any single question or group of questions

5. Note and underline key words – *all, most, fewest, least, best, worst, same, opposite,* etc.
6. Pay particular attention to negatives
7. Note unusual option, e.g., unduly long, short, complex, different or similar in content to the body of the question
8. Observe the use of "hedging" words – *probably, may, most likely,* etc.
9. Make sure that your answer is put next to the same number as the question
10. Do not second-guess unless you have good reason to believe the second answer is definitely more correct
11. Cross out original answer if you decide another answer is more accurate; do not erase until you are ready to hand your paper in
12. Answer all questions; guess unless instructed otherwise
13. Leave time for review

    b. Essay questions
      1. Read each question carefully
      2. Determine exactly what is wanted. Underline key words or phrases.
      3. Decide on outline or paragraph answer
      4. Include many different points and elements unless asked to develop any one or two points or elements
      5. Show impartiality by giving pros and cons unless directed to select one side only
      6. Make and write down any assumptions you find necessary to answer the questions
      7. Watch your English, grammar, punctuation and choice of words
      8. Time your answers; don't crowd material

8) Answering the essay question

Most essay questions can be answered by framing the specific response around several key words or ideas. Here are a few such key words or ideas:

M's: manpower, materials, methods, money, management
P's: purpose, program, policy, plan, procedure, practice, problems, pitfalls, personnel, public relations

    a. Six basic steps in handling problems:
      1. Preliminary plan and background development
      2. Collect information, data and facts
      3. Analyze and interpret information, data and facts
      4. Analyze and develop solutions as well as make recommendations
      5. Prepare report and sell recommendations
      6. Install recommendations and follow up effectiveness

    b. Pitfalls to avoid
      1. *Taking things for granted* – A statement of the situation does not necessarily imply that each of the elements is necessarily true; for example, a complaint may be invalid and biased so that all that can be taken for granted is that a complaint has been registered

2. *Considering only one side of a situation* – Wherever possible, indicate several alternatives and then point out the reasons you selected the best one
3. *Failing to indicate follow up* – Whenever your answer indicates action on your part, make certain that you will take proper follow-up action to see how successful your recommendations, procedures or actions turn out to be
4. *Taking too long in answering any single question* – Remember to time your answers properly

IX. AFTER THE TEST

Scoring procedures differ in detail among civil service jurisdictions although the general principles are the same. Whether the papers are hand-scored or graded by machine we have described, they are nearly always graded by number. That is, the person who marks the paper knows only the number – never the name – of the applicant. Not until all the papers have been graded will they be matched with names. If other tests, such as training and experience or oral interview ratings have been given, scores will be combined. Different parts of the examination usually have different weights. For example, the written test might count 60 percent of the final grade, and a rating of training and experience 40 percent. In many jurisdictions, veterans will have a certain number of points added to their grades.

After the final grade has been determined, the names are placed in grade order and an eligible list is established. There are various methods for resolving ties between those who get the same final grade – probably the most common is to place first the name of the person whose application was received first. Job offers are made from the eligible list in the order the names appear on it. You will be notified of your grade and your rank as soon as all these computations have been made. This will be done as rapidly as possible.

People who are found to meet the requirements in the announcement are called "eligibles." Their names are put on a list of eligible candidates. An eligible's chances of getting a job depend on how high he stands on this list and how fast agencies are filling jobs from the list.

When a job is to be filled from a list of eligibles, the agency asks for the names of people on the list of eligibles for that job. When the civil service commission receives this request, it sends to the agency the names of the three people highest on this list. Or, if the job to be filled has specialized requirements, the office sends the agency the names of the top three persons who meet these requirements from the general list.

The appointing officer makes a choice from among the three people whose names were sent to him. If the selected person accepts the appointment, the names of the others are put back on the list to be considered for future openings.

That is the rule in hiring from all kinds of eligible lists, whether they are for typist, carpenter, chemist, or something else. For every vacancy, the appointing officer has his choice of any one of the top three eligibles on the list. This explains why the person whose name is on top of the list sometimes does not get an appointment when some of the persons lower on the list do. If the appointing officer chooses the second or third eligible, the No. 1 eligible does not get a job at once, but stays on the list until he is appointed or the list is terminated.

X. HOW TO PASS THE INTERVIEW TEST

The examination for which you applied requires an oral interview test. You have already taken the written test and you are now being called for the interview test – the final part of the formal examination.

You may think that it is not possible to prepare for an interview test and that there are no procedures to follow during an interview. Our purpose is to point out some things you can do in advance that will help you and some good rules to follow and pitfalls to avoid while you are being interviewed.

What is an interview supposed to test?

The written examination is designed to test the technical knowledge and competence of the candidate; the oral is designed to evaluate intangible qualities, not readily measured otherwise, and to establish a list showing the relative fitness of each candidate – as measured against his competitors – for the position sought. Scoring is not on the basis of "right" and "wrong," but on a sliding scale of values ranging from "not passable" to "outstanding." As a matter of fact, it is possible to achieve a relatively low score without a single "incorrect" answer because of evident weakness in the qualities being measured.

Occasionally, an examination may consist entirely of an oral test – either an individual or a group oral. In such cases, information is sought concerning the technical knowledges and abilities of the candidate, since there has been no written examination for this purpose. More commonly, however, an oral test is used to supplement a written examination.

Who conducts interviews?

The composition of oral boards varies among different jurisdictions. In nearly all, a representative of the personnel department serves as chairman. One of the members of the board may be a representative of the department in which the candidate would work. In some cases, "outside experts" are used, and, frequently, a businessman or some other representative of the general public is asked to serve. Labor and management or other special groups may be represented. The aim is to secure the services of experts in the appropriate field.

However the board is composed, it is a good idea (and not at all improper or unethical) to ascertain in advance of the interview who the members are and what groups they represent. When you are introduced to them, you will have some idea of their backgrounds and interests, and at least you will not stutter and stammer over their names.

What should be done before the interview?

While knowledge about the board members is useful and takes some of the surprise element out of the interview, there is other preparation which is more substantive. It *is* possible to prepare for an oral interview – in several ways:

1) Keep a copy of your application and review it carefully before the interview

This may be the only document before the oral board, and the starting point of the interview. Know what education and experience you have listed there, and the sequence and dates of all of it. Sometimes the board will ask you to review the highlights of your experience for them; you should not have to hem and haw doing it.

2) Study the class specification and the examination announcement

Usually, the oral board has one or both of these to guide them. The qualities, characteristics or knowledges required by the position sought are stated in these documents. They offer valuable clues as to the nature of the oral interview. For example, if the job involves supervisory responsibilities, the announcement will usually indicate that knowledge of modern supervisory methods and the qualifications of the candidate as a supervisor will be tested. If so, you can expect such questions, frequently in the form of a hypothetical situation which you are expected to solve. NEVER go into an oral without knowledge of the duties and responsibilities of the job you seek.

3) Think through each qualification required

Try to visualize the kind of questions you would ask if you were a board member. How well could you answer them? Try especially to appraise your own knowledge and background in each area, *measured against the job sought*, and identify any areas in which you are weak. Be critical and realistic – do not flatter yourself.

4) Do some general reading in areas in which you feel you may be weak

For example, if the job involves supervision and your past experience has NOT, some general reading in supervisory methods and practices, particularly in the field of human relations, might be useful. Do NOT study agency procedures or detailed manuals. The oral board will be testing your understanding and capacity, not your memory.

5) Get a good night's sleep and watch your general health and mental attitude

You will want a clear head at the interview. Take care of a cold or any other minor ailment, and of course, no hangovers.

What should be done on the day of the interview?

Now comes the day of the interview itself. Give yourself plenty of time to get there. Plan to arrive somewhat ahead of the scheduled time, particularly if your appointment is in the fore part of the day. If a previous candidate fails to appear, the board might be ready for you a bit early. By early afternoon an oral board is almost invariably behind schedule if there are many candidates, and you may have to wait. Take along a book or magazine to read, or your application to review, but leave any extraneous material in the waiting room when you go in for your interview. In any event, relax and compose yourself.

The matter of dress is important. The board is forming impressions about you – from your experience, your manners, your attitude, and your appearance. Give your personal appearance careful attention. Dress your best, but not your flashiest. Choose conservative, appropriate clothing, and be sure it is immaculate. This is a business interview, and your appearance should indicate that you regard it as such. Besides, being well groomed and properly dressed will help boost your confidence.

Sooner or later, someone will call your name and escort you into the interview room. *This is it.* From here on you are on your own. It is too late for any more preparation. But remember, you asked for this opportunity to prove your fitness, and you are here because your request was granted.

What happens when you go in?

The usual sequence of events will be as follows: The clerk (who is often the board stenographer) will introduce you to the chairman of the oral board, who will introduce you to the other members of the board. Acknowledge the introductions before you sit down. Do not be surprised if you find a microphone facing you or a stenotypist sitting by. Oral interviews are usually recorded in the event of an appeal or other review.

Usually the chairman of the board will open the interview by reviewing the highlights of your education and work experience from your application – primarily for the benefit of the other members of the board, as well as to get the material into the record. Do not interrupt or comment unless there is an error or significant misinterpretation; if that is the case, do not hesitate. But do not quibble about insignificant matters. Also, he will usually ask you some question about your education, experience or your present job – partly to get you to start talking and to establish the interviewing "rapport." He may start the actual questioning, or turn it over to one of the other members. Frequently, each member undertakes the questioning on a particular area, one in which he is perhaps most competent, so you can expect each member to participate in the examination. Because time is limited, you may also expect some rather abrupt switches in the direction the questioning takes, so do not be upset by it. Normally, a board member will not pursue a single line of questioning unless he discovers a particular strength or weakness.

After each member has participated, the chairman will usually ask whether any member has any further questions, then will ask you if you have anything you wish to add. Unless you are expecting this question, it may floor you. Worse, it may start you off on an extended, extemporaneous speech. The board is not usually seeking more information. The question is principally to offer you a last opportunity to present further qualifications or to indicate that you have nothing to add. So, if you feel that a significant qualification or characteristic has been overlooked, it is proper to point it out in a sentence or so. Do not compliment the board on the thoroughness of their examination – they have been sketchy, and you know it. If you wish, merely say, "No thank you, I have nothing further to add." This is a point where you can "talk yourself out" of a good impression or fail to present an important bit of information. Remember, *you close the interview yourself*.

The chairman will then say, "That is all, Mr. _____, thank you." Do not be startled; the interview is over, and quicker than you think. Thank him, gather your belongings and take your leave. Save your sigh of relief for the other side of the door.

How to put your best foot forward

Throughout this entire process, you may feel that the board individually and collectively is trying to pierce your defenses, seek out your hidden weaknesses and embarrass and confuse you. Actually, this is not true. They are obliged to make an appraisal of your qualifications for the job you are seeking, and they want to see you in your best light. Remember, they must interview all candidates and a non-cooperative candidate may become a failure in spite of their best efforts to bring out his qualifications. Here are 15 suggestions that will help you:

1) Be natural – Keep your attitude confident, not cocky

If you are not confident that you can do the job, do not expect the board to be. Do not apologize for your weaknesses, try to bring out your strong points. The board is interested in a positive, not negative, presentation. Cockiness will antagonize any board member and make him wonder if you are covering up a weakness by a false show of strength.

2) Get comfortable, but don't lounge or sprawl

Sit erectly but not stiffly. A careless posture may lead the board to conclude that you are careless in other things, or at least that you are not impressed by the importance of the occasion. Either conclusion is natural, even if incorrect. Do not fuss with your clothing, a pencil or an ashtray. Your hands may occasionally be useful to emphasize a point; do not let them become a point of distraction.

3) Do not wisecrack or make small talk

This is a serious situation, and your attitude should show that you consider it as such. Further, the time of the board is limited – they do not want to waste it, and neither should you.

4) Do not exaggerate your experience or abilities

In the first place, from information in the application or other interviews and sources, the board may know more about you than you think. Secondly, you probably will not get away with it. An experienced board is rather adept at spotting such a situation, so do not take the chance.

5) If you know a board member, do not make a point of it, yet do not hide it

Certainly you are not fooling him, and probably not the other members of the board. Do not try to take advantage of your acquaintanceship – it will probably do you little good.

6) Do not dominate the interview

Let the board do that. They will give you the clues – do not assume that you have to do all the talking. Realize that the board has a number of questions to ask you, and do not try to take up all the interview time by showing off your extensive knowledge of the answer to the first one.

7) Be attentive

You only have 20 minutes or so, and you should keep your attention at its sharpest throughout. When a member is addressing a problem or question to you, give him your undivided attention. Address your reply principally to him, but do not exclude the other board members.

8) Do not interrupt

A board member may be stating a problem for you to analyze. He will ask you a question when the time comes. Let him state the problem, and wait for the question.

9) Make sure you understand the question

Do not try to answer until you are sure what the question is. If it is not clear, restate it in your own words or ask the board member to clarify it for you. However, do not haggle about minor elements.

10) Reply promptly but not hastily

A common entry on oral board rating sheets is "candidate responded readily," or "candidate hesitated in replies." Respond as promptly and quickly as you can, but do not jump to a hasty, ill-considered answer.

11) Do not be peremptory in your answers

A brief answer is proper – but do not fire your answer back. That is a losing game from your point of view. The board member can probably ask questions much faster than you can answer them.

12) Do not try to create the answer you think the board member wants

He is interested in what kind of mind you have and how it works – not in playing games. Furthermore, he can usually spot this practice and will actually grade you down on it.

13) Do not switch sides in your reply merely to agree with a board member

Frequently, a member will take a contrary position merely to draw you out and to see if you are willing and able to defend your point of view. Do not start a debate, yet do not surrender a good position. If a position is worth taking, it is worth defending.

14) Do not be afraid to admit an error in judgment if you are shown to be wrong

The board knows that you are forced to reply without any opportunity for careful consideration. Your answer may be demonstrably wrong. If so, admit it and get on with the interview.

15) Do not dwell at length on your present job

The opening question may relate to your present assignment. Answer the question but do not go into an extended discussion. You are being examined for a *new* job, not your present one. As a matter of fact, try to phrase ALL your answers in terms of the job for which you are being examined.

Basis of Rating

Probably you will forget most of these "do's" and "don'ts" when you walk into the oral interview room. Even remembering them all will not ensure you a passing grade. Perhaps you did not have the qualifications in the first place. But remembering them will help you to put your best foot forward, without treading on the toes of the board members.

Rumor and popular opinion to the contrary notwithstanding, an oral board wants you to make the best appearance possible. They know you are under pressure – but they also want to see how you respond to it as a guide to what your reaction would be under the pressures of the job you seek. They will be influenced by the degree of poise you display, the personal traits you show and the manner in which you respond.

ABOUT THIS BOOK

This book contains tests divided into Examination Sections. Go through each test, answering every question in the margin. We have also attached a sample answer sheet at the back of the book that can be removed and used. At the end of each test look at the answer key and check your answers. On the ones you got wrong, look at the right answer choice and learn. Do not fill in the answers first. Do not memorize the questions and answers, but understand the answer and principles involved. On your test, the questions will likely be different from the samples. Questions are changed and new ones added. If you understand these past questions you should have success with any changes that arise. Tests may consist of several types of questions. We have additional books on each subject should more study be advisable or necessary for you. Finally, the more you study, the better prepared you will be. This book is intended to be the last thing you study before you walk into the examination room. Prior study of relevant texts is also recommended. NLC publishes some of these in our Fundamental Series. Knowledge and good sense are important factors in passing your exam. Good luck also helps. So now study this Passbook, absorb the material contained within and take that knowledge into the examination. Then do your best to pass that exam.

EXAMINATION SECTION

EXAMINATION SECTION
TEST 1

DIRECTIONS: Each question or incomplete statement is followed by several suggested answers or completions. Select the one that BEST answers the question or completes the statement. *PRINT THE LETTER OF THE CORRECT ANSWER IN THE SPACE AT THE RIGHT.*

1. With regard to the requirement of the auditing standard that sufficient and competent evidential matter be obtained, the term competent PRIMARILY refers to the evidence.
   A. consistency
   B. relevance
   C. measurability
   D. dependability

   1._____

2. Audit working papers should NOT
   A. include any client-prepared papers or documents other than those prepared by the auditor
   B. be kept by the auditor after review and completion of the audit except for items required for the income tax return
   C. be submitted to the client to support the financial statements and to provide evidence of the audit work performed
   D. by themselves be expected to provide sufficient support for the auditor's operation

   2._____

3. Mr. Jason Stone operates a small drugstore as an individual proprietor. During the past year, his books were not properly kept. He asks you, as a CPA, to give him some advice concerning the earnings of his business during the calendar year 2011. A review of his bank accounts and a diary of financial data reveal the information presented below:
   Deposits made during 2018 per bank statements totaled $226,000. Deposits include investments made by Mr. Shea as well as a loan he obtained from the bank for $25,000. Disbursements during 2018 per bank statement totaled $185,000. Included are personal withdrawals of $15,000 and payments on debt of $10,000.
   Net equity of Jason Stone at January 1, 2018 was determined to be $45,000.
   Net equity of Jason Stone at December 31, 2018 was determined to be $75,000.
   During 2018, funds invested by Jason Stone in the business amounted to $6,500.
   Based upon the *net worth* method, net income for the year ended December, 2018 was
   A. $35,000   B. $38,500   C. $40,000   D. $42,000

   3._____

4. Because of past association, a senior accountant is convinced of the competence and honesty of those who prepared the financial information which he is auditing. He consequently concludes that certain verification procedures are unnecessary.
   This conclusion by the senior accountant is ill-advised for the proper performance of his present audit MAINLY because the
   A. members of the staff often lack the specialized skills and training without which verification in an audit cannot proceed
   B. verification procedures depend upon the materiality of the subject matter under examination and not upon the personal characteristics of the individuals involved
   C. nature of opinion expressed in the report issued by the senior accountant, at the end of his audit, is grounded on personal considerations
   D. quality of the senior accountant's independence and his objective examination of the information under review is impaired

   4._____

5. Of the following statement ratios, the one that represents *a growth ratio is*
    A. working capital ratio
    B. acid-test ratio
    C. long-term debt to total capitalization
    D. dollar earnings per share

Questions-6-8.

DIRECTIONS: Questions 6 through 8 are to be answered on the basis of the information given below.

During the course of an examinations of the financial statements of a wholesale establishment, the following facts were revealed for the year ended December 3, 2018:

I. Although merchandise: inventory costing $3,000 was on hand and was-included in the inventory count on December 31, 2018, title had passed and it was billed to the customer on December 31, 2018 at a sale price of $4,500.
II. Merchandise had been billed to the customer on December 31, 2018 in the amount of $5,200 but had not been shipped to him. This merchandise which cost $3,500, was not included in the inventory at the end of the year. The goods were shipped and title passed on January 15, 2019.
III. Merchandise costing $6,000 was recorded as a purchase on December 31, 2018 but was Not included in the inventory at that date.
IV. Merchandise costing $5,000 was received on January 3, 2019, but was recorded on the books as of December 31, 2018, and included in inventory as of December 31, 2018. The goods were shipped on December 30, 2018 by the vendor F.O.B. shipping point.
V. An examination of receiving records indicated that merchandise costing $7,000 was received on December 31, 2018. It was included in inventory as of that date but not recorded as a purchase.

6. Adjustments to correct the inventory figure will reflect a net adjustment so as to
    A. reduce it by $6,500   B. increase it by $6,500
    C. reduce it by $8,000   D. increase it by $8,000

7. Adjustments to correct the sales figure will result in a net adjustment to sales of a (n)
    A. increase by $5,200   B. decrease by $5,200
    C. increase by $6,300   D. decrease by $6,300

8. The net adjustment to purchases for the period ending December 31, 2018 will result in a(n)
    A. increase of $4,000   B. decrease of $7,000
    C. increase of $7,000   D. decrease of $4,000

Questions 9-10.

DIRECTIONS: Questions 9 and 10 are to be answered on the basis of the information given below.

A company worth $500,000 of common capital stock, par value $100 per share with retained earnings of $100,000, decides to change its capitalization from a par to a no-par basis. It, therefore, called in its 5,000 shares of par value stock and issued in place thereof 10,000 shares of no-par value stock.

9. The balance in the capital stock account after the change is   9._____
   A. $1,000,000   B. $500,000
   C. $,400,000   D. $200,000

10. The balance in the retained earnings account after the change is   10._____
    A. $90,000   B. $100,000   C. $125,000   D. $250,000

11. Among the assets on the December 31, 2018 balance sheet of the Wolf Corporation   11._____
    was the following:
    Investment in Sheep Company
    1,000 shares @ $90 bought January 1, 2018 $90,000
    The net worth section of the balance sheet of the Sheep Company on the same date
    was as follows:

    NET WORTH
    Capital Stock, 1,000 shares $100,000
    Deficit January 1, 2018 $20,000
       Less Operating Profit 2018   15,000
    Deficit December 31, 2018   5,000
    Total Net worth $ 95,000

    The net debit or credit to Consolidated Surplus arising from consolidation of the
    Sheep Company with the parent Wolf Corporation is
    A. $3,000 credit   B. $5,000 credit
    C. $7,000 debit   D. $10,000 credit

Questions 12-15.

DIRECTIONS: Questions 12 through 15 are to be answered on the basis of the
            Trial Balances and the Notes below.

CLIMAX CORPORATION - Trial Balances (000 Omitted)

	December 31, 2018		December 31, 2017	
	Debit	Credit	Debit	Credit
Cash	$ 178		$ 84	
Accounts Receivable	300		240	
Allowance for Bad Debts		$ 13		$ 10
Merchandise Inventory	370		400	
Building & Equipment	420		360	
Allowance for Depreciation		180		190
Accounts Payable		220		210
Mortgage Bonds		300		300
Unamortized Bond Discount	18			21
Capital Stock		357		270
Retained Earnings		125		90
Net Sales		$4,200		$4,000
Cost of Goods Sold	$2,300		$2,100	
Salaries & Wages	1,500		1,400	
Heat & Utilities	110		100	
Depreciation	20		20	
Taxes & Insurance	10		10	
Interest	16		15	
Bad Debts	20		20	
Losso on Equipment Sales (Note 1)	6		—	
Dividends Paid (Note 2)	127		300	
	$5,395	$5,395	$5,070	$5,070

NOTES: (1) In 2018 equipment costing $40,000 and having a net bookvalue of $10,000 was sold for $4,000.
(2) Dividends paid in 2018 include a stock dividend of $27,000.

12. The net change in working capital from 2017 to 2018 is   12.____
    A. $111,000   B. $130,000   C. $260,000   D. $333,000

13. The amount of funds provided from net income for the year ended December 31, 2018 is   13.____
    A. $214,000   B. $244,000   C. $254,000   D. $284,000

14. The amount of funds applied to dividends during the year 2018 is   14.____
    A. $100,000   B. $125,000   C. $175,000   D. $202,350

15. The amount of funds applied to building and equipment during the year 2018 is   15.____
    A. $100,000   B. $70,000   C. $50,000   D. $30,000

Questions 16-17.

DIRECTIONS: Questions 16 and 17 are to be answered on the basis of the information given below.
The Natural Sales Company issues gift certificates in denominations of $5, $10 and $25. They are redeemable in merchandise having a markup of 30% of Selling Price.

During December, $35,000 of gift certificates was sold and $20,000 was redeemed. It is estimated that 5% of the certificates issued will never be redeemed.

16. The PROPER entry to reflect the current liability with respect to these certificates is   16.____
    A. $13,250   B. $14,250   C. $15,250   D. $16,250

17. The cost of the merchandise issued to meet the redeemed certificates is   17.____
    A. $11,000   B. $13,000   C. $14,000   D. $17,000

Questions 18-19.

DIRECTIONS: Questions 18 and 19 are to be answered on the basis of the information given below.
Arthur Evans commenced business in 2017 but did not maintain a complete set of proper records. He relied on the bank statements in order to compute his income. All his receipts Are deposited, and all his expenditures are made by check.
His bank statements and other records reflected the following:

Bank balance per bank 12/31/2017	$ 14,735
Bank balance per bank 12/31/2018	18,380
Deposits for 2018 per bank statement	209,450
Deposits in transit 12/31/2017	3,590
Deposits in transit 12/31/2018	4,150

Checks returned with the January 2018 bank statement showed a total of $4,770 checks issued in 2018.
2018 checks not returned by the bank at December 31, 2018 amounted to $5,150.
$6,430 of checks were issued in 2018 in payment of purchases made in 2017.
$9,425 of deposits was made by Mr. Evans in 2018 representing 2017 sales.

Unpaid bills for 2018 amounted to $2,150 on December 31, 2018.

Accounts Receivable for 2018 on December 31, 2018 were $10,930.
Merchandise inventory figures on the following dates were:
    December 31, 2017 $13,000
    December 31, 2018   17,580

On July 1, 2018, machinery costing $8,000 was purchased. The estimated life was 5 years with a salvage value of $500.

18. The balance of the cash in the bank according to the books on December 31, 2018 was   18.____
    A. $18,380   B. $17,380   C. $16,380   D. $15,380

19. The Sales Revenue for 2018 was   19.____
    A. $211,515   B. $209,515   C. $208,515   D. $207,515

Questions 20-21.

DIRECTIONS: Questions 20 and 21 are to be answered on the basis of the information given below.

In the examination of an imprest petty cash fund of $600, you were presented with the following fund composition shown below. The date of examining the petty cash fund was the balance sheet date.

Currency - bills	$310.00
Cash - coins	3.15
Postage stamps	50.00
Sales returns memos for cash refunded to customers	15.50
Check of one employee dated one month in advance	75.00
Vouchers for miscellaneous office expenses	100.85
Sales slip of an employee who purchased company merchandise; the money in payment was taken from the fund, entered as cash sale, and the sales slip inserted in the fund	45.50

20. The corrected balance of petty cash for balance sheet purposes is   20.____
    A. $313.15   B. $319.32   C. $347.53   D. $409.27

21. A correcting journal entry to establish the correct fund balance would increase expenses by   21.____
    A. $100.85   B. $212.31   C. $28.28   D. $139.50

22. The PRIMARY objective of an audit, as generally understood in accounting practice, is to   22.____
    A. assert a series of claims for management as to the financial condition of the company
    B. establish the reliability or unreliability as to the financial statements and supporting accounting records of the company
    C. install special procedures involved in the periodic closing of the accounts prior to the preparation of financial statements of the company
    D. summarize accounts and financial transactions to determine the costs of processes or units of production for the company

Questions 23-25.

DIRECTIONS: Questions 23 through 25 are to be answered on the basis of the information given below.

The following data related to the business operations for the calendar years 2016, 2017, and 2018 of the Wholly Corporation.

	2016	2017	2018
Net income per books	$170,000	$190,000	$140,000
Dividends	15,000	20,000	10,000
Purchases made in year 2017 recorded as purchased in 2018 but recorded in inventory in 2017		25,000	
Inventory value December 31, 2018 underestimated			5,000
Depreciation omitted -			
applicable to 2016	3,000		
applicable to 2017		4,500	
applicable to 2018			6,000
Overstatement of prepaid advertising as of January 1, 2017		1,500	
Salaries - earned during 2016 paid during 2017 - no accruals	18,000		
Payroll taxes on salarie	1,440		

23. The net profit for 2016 after adjusting for the facts given above is
    A. $146,060   B. $150,050   C. $164,200   D. $192,835   23._____

24. The net profit for 2017 after adjusting for facts given
    A. $152,400   B. $165,700   C. $173,145   D. $181,440   24._____

25. If the balance of the retained earnings account was $265,000 on January 1, 2016, the balance of the retainedearnings account on December 31, 2018 after corrections is   25._____
    A. $711,500   B. $525,000   C. $424,360   D. $307,420

Questions 26-30.

DIRECTIONS: Each question numbered 26 through 30 consists of a description of a transaction that indicates a two fold change on the balance sheet. Each of these transactions may be classified under one of the following categories. Examine each question carefully. In the correspondingly numbered space at the right, mark the appropriate space for the letter preceding the category below which BEST represents the charges that should be made on the balance sheet, as of December 31, 2017.

A. Current Assets are *overstated* and Retained Earnings are *overstated*
B. Current Assets are *understated* and Retained Earnings are *understated*
C. Current Liabilities are *overstated* and Retained Earnings are *overstated*
D. Current Liabilities are *understated* and Retained Earnings are *overstated*

26. Goods shipped on consignment out were not included in the final inventory although the entries were properly made for such consignments.

27. A number of cash sales made subsequent to the balance sheet date were recorded as sales in the prior period before the balance sheet date. The merchandise was included in inventories.

28. A cash dividend declared December 21, 2017, payable on January 15, 2018 to stockholders of record as of December 28, 2017, had not been recorded as of December 31, 2017.

29. The provision for the allowance for doubtful accounts receivable for the current period that should have been made had not been recorded.

30. Merchandise received by December 31, 2017, and properly included in inventory on that date, was not entered as a purchase until January 2018.

Questions 31-33.

DIRECTIONS: Questions 31 through 33 are to be answered on the basis of the information given below.

Ten men work as a group on a particular manufacturing operation. When the weekly production of the group exceeds a standard number of pieces per hour, each man in the group is paid a bonus for the excess production; the bonus is in addition to his wages at the hourly rate. The amount of the bonus is computed by first determining the percentage by which the groups production exceeds the standard. One-half of this percentage is then applied to a wage rate of $1.25 to determine an hourly bonus rate. Each man in the group is paid, as a bonus, the bonus rate applied to his total hours worked during the week. The standard rate of production before a bonus can be earned is two hundred pieces per hour.

The production record for a given week was: Hours Worked Production

Days	Hours worked	Production
Monday	72	17,680
Tuesday	72	17,348
Wednesday	72	18,800
Thuresday	72	18,560
Friday	71.5	17,888
Saturday	40	9,600
	399.5	99,076

31. The rate of the bonus for the week is _____ %.
    A. 24   B. 20   C. 18   D. 12

32. The bonus paid to the ten-man group for the week is
    A. $59.93   B. $69.39   C. $95.00   D. $225.00

33. The total wages of one employee who worked 40 hours at a base rate of $1.00 per hour are
    A. $46   B. $50   C. $54   D. $58

34. A junior accountant reported to his senior that he had performed the operations listed below.
Which one of the following statements about these operations CORRECTLY describes the operation?
   A. Vouchered the amount of petty cash
   B. Vouchered the receivables ledger accounts with the sales register
   C. Analyzed the fixed assets account
   D. Checked all entries in the general journal to original evidence

35. Sales during July 2018 for the Major Company were $267,500, of which $170,000 was on account. The sales figure presented to you includes the total sales tax charged to retail customers (assume a sales tax rate of 7%).
The sales tax liability that should be shown at the end of July 2018 is
   A. $8,300
   B. $9,400
   C. $17,500
   D. $18,750

Questions 36-37.

DIRECTIONS: Questions 36 and 37 are to be answered on the basis of the information given below.

During the audit of records of the Short Corporation for the year ended December 31, 2018, the auditor was presented with the following information:

The finished goods inventory consisted of 22,000 units carried at a cost of $17,600 at December 31, 2018. The finished goods inventory at the beginning of the year (January 1, 2018) consisted of 24,000 units, priced at a cost of $16,800. During the year, 4,000 units were manufactured at a cost of $3,600 and 6,000 units were sold.

36. To PROPERLY reflect the cost of the finished goods inventory at December 31, 2018, if the FIFO method was used, assuming there was no work-in-process inventory, would require an adjustment of
   A. $1,400 credit   B. $1,400 debit   C. $1,600 credit   D. $1,600 debit

37. To PROPERLY reflect the cost of the finished goods inventory at December 31, 2018 if the LIFO method was used, assuming there was no work-in-process Inventory, would require an adjustment of
   A. $2,200 debit   B. $2,200 credit   C. $4,200 credit   D. $4,200 debit

38. Within the general field of auditing, there are internal auditors and independent auditors who differ significantly one from the other in that the latter group:

   A. is responsible for a more complete, detailed examination of accounting data
   B. conduct standard audits established by custom and usage for a particular trade or industry
   C. direct their investigations primarily to matters of fraud and criminal misrepresentation
   D. issue reports for the benefit of other interests, such as shareholders and creditors

9 (#1)

39. Moreland Corporation sells merchandise at a gross profit of 25% of sales. Fire on the premises of this Corporation on July 16, 2018 resulted in the destruction of the merchandise. The Corporation's merchandise is insured against fire by a $150,000 insurance policy with an 80% co-insurance clause. The Corporation's records show the following:

    Sales -- January 1, 2018 to July 16, 2018 $400,000
    Inventory -- January 1, 2018 $ 65,000
    Purchases -- January 1, 2018 to July 16, 2018 $460,000
    Merchandise salvaged $ 25,000

The amount of inventory destroyed by fire is
    A. $150,000   B. $200,000   C. $225,000   D. $300,000

40. Below are the totals of the cash receipts and disbursement books of the Small Corporation for the calendar year 2018
    Receipts $392,369.72
    Disbursements $331,477.87

The bank balance on January 1, 2018 was $38,610.21. The bank balance on December 31, 2018 was $101,918.34. No checks were outstanding on January 1, 2018. Checks outstanding on December 31, 2018 amounted to $5,416.28. Undeposited checks on hand December 31, 2018 were $3,000 which are included in the December cash receipts. Bank deposits for the year total $387,643.72.

The total SHORTAGE in cash is
    A. $1,726   B. $2,416.28   C. $3,000   D. $3,452

41. A state corporation, all of whose business is done within the city, showed the following for 2018:
    Entire net income $ 1,000
    Salaries to Officers deducted in
      determining entire net income $ 40,000
    Average capital $450,000

The corporation's city business tax payable (assuming a 7% rate on income and a .001 rate on capital) is
    A. $546   B. $450   C. $70   D. $25

42. Sales revenue serves as the basis for determining _____ taxes.
    A. estate   B. excise   C. payroll   D. property.

43. ABC Corporation operates in the city and would be subjected to the following taxes:
    I. Federal Corporation Income Tax – Surtax 26% and Normal Tax 22%
    II. State Franchise Tax - 72%

If income before taxes for 2018 was $370,000 per the federal tax return (after establishing estimate), assuming the rates as noted above, the tax liabilities that should be set up are Federal and State.
    A. $180,000; $25,800   B. $177,600; $29,700
    C. $165,500; $20,000   D. $171,100; $30,000

44. In the examination of a manufacturing company where inventory values are of a material amount, the client has restricted the extent of the independent CPA's audit examination of his records by not permitting the CPA to observe the taking of inventory at the close of the company's fiscal year. In such a case, which of the following opinions with regard to the audit report would be APPROPRIATE?_____opinion.
    A. Unqualified
    B. Qualified
    C. Adverse
    D. Disclaimer of

45. Accounting data are subject to error from a variety of sources and for a variety of reasons. Of the following, the MOST efficient way to lessen this problem is to
    A. identify and classify errors as to type and kind as soon as they are detected
    B. provide for machine calculation of accounting data wherever possible
    C. confirm accounting data by independent third parties
    D. designate an individual to be responsible for the accuracy of accounting data

46. Normally, an auditor does NOT rely upon his study and testing of a system of internal control to
    A. evaluate the reliability of the system
    B. uncover embezzlements of the client's system
    C. help determine the scope of other auditing procedures to be followed
    D. gain support for his opinion as to the accuracy and fairness of the financial statements

Questions 47-50.

DIRECTIONS: Questions 47 through 50 are to be answered on the basis of the information given below.

An office clerk who was not familiar with proper accounting procedures prepared the following financial report for the Dunrite Corporation as of June 30, 2018. In addition to the errors in presentation, additional data below were not considered in the preparation of the report. Restate this balance sheet in proper form, giving recognition to the additional data so that you will be able to determine the required information to answer these questions.

DUNRITE CORPORATION
June 30, 2018

CURRENT ASSETS			
Cash			$155,000
Marketable securities			82,400
Investment in affiliated company.			175,000
Treasury stock		$ 25,500	
Less reserve for trea		25,500	
Accounts receivable		$ 277,800	
Accounts payable		135,000	142,800
Total current assets			$ 555,200
PLANT ASSETS			
Equipment		$ 450,000	
Building	$400,000		
Reserve for plant expansion	100,000	300,000	
Land.		50,000	
Goodwill		35,000	
Prepaid expenses		12,000	847,000
Total Assets			$1,402,200

11 (#1)

LIABILITIES
Cash dividend payable		$25,000	
Stock dividend payable		15,000	
Accrued liabilities		15,700	
Bonds payable	$400,000		
Sinking fund	325,000	75,000	
Total Current Liabilities			$ 130,700

STOCKHOLDERS' EQUITY
Paid-in capital			
Common stock		$550,000	
Retained earnings and reserves			
Premium common stock	$74,000		
Reserve - doubtful accounts	7,500		
Reserve - depreciation of equipment	140,000		
Reserve - depreciation building	170,000		
Reserve - income-taxes	50,000		
Retained earnings	280,000	$721,500	
Total Liabilities and Equity			$1,402,200

ADDITIONAL DATA:
  A. The reserve for income taxes represents the balance due on the estimated liability for taxes on income of the current fiscal year.
  B. Marketable securities are recorded at cost and have a market value at June 30, 2018 of $81,000. They represent temporary investments.
  C. The investment in the affiliated company is a minority interest carried at cost.
  D. Bonds payable are due 10 years from the balance-sheet date.
  E. The stock dividend payable was declared on June 30, 2018.

47. After restatement of the balance sheet in proper form, and giving recognition to 47.____
The additional data, the Total Current Assets would be
   A. $509,200   B. $519,700   C. $610,000   D. $735,000

48. After restatement of the balance sheet in proper form, and giving recognition to the 48.____
Additional data, the Total Current Liabilities would be
   A. $225,700   B. $325,200   C. $352,700   D. $480,000

49. After restatement of the balance sheet in proper form, and giving recognition to the 49.____
additional data, the Stockholders' Equity shows a total of
   A. $730,100   B. $819,000   C. $910,000   D. $1,019,000

50. After restatement of the balance sheet in proper form, and giving recognition to the 50.____
additional data, the net book value of the total plant equipment would be
   A. $440,000   B. $590,000   C. $750,000   D. $850,000

KEY (CORRECT ANSWERS)

1. D	26. B
2. C	27. A
3. B	28. D
4. D	29. A
5. D	30. D
6. B	31. D
7. B	32. A
8. C	33. A
9. B	34. C
10. B	35. C
11. D	36. A
12. A	37. B
13. B	38. D
14. A	39. B
15. A	40. A
16. A	41. A
17. C	42. B
18. B	43. D
19. A	44. D
20. A	45. C
21. A	46. B
22. B	47. B
23. A	48. A
24. D	49. D
25. A	50. B

TEST 2

DIRECTIONS: Each question or incomplete statement is followed by several suggested answers or completions. Select the one that BEST answers the question or completes the statement. *PRINT THE LETTER OF THE CORRECT ANSWER IN THE SPACE AT THE RIGHT.*

Question 1.

DIRECTIONS: Question 1 is based on the following portion of an income tax withholding table. In answering this question, assume that this table was in effect for the full year.

If the payroll period with respect to an employee is daily:

And the wages are		And the number of witholding exemptions claimed is				
At least	But less than	0	1	2	3	4
		The amount of income tax to be withheld shall be				
$172	$176	$24.40	$20.80	$17.20	$13.60	$10.00
176	180	24.90	21.30	17.70	14.20	10.60
180	184	25.50	18.30	18.30	14.70	11.10

1. K received a daily wage of $176.40 the first 7 pay periods and $182.50 the last 19 pay periods. He claimed 3 exemptions the first 9 pay periods and 4 the rest of the year. Total income tax withheld during the year was
   A. $288.10
   B. $295.30
   C. $316.50
   D. $317.50
   E. none of the above

   1.____

2. A voucher contained the following items:
   6 desks @ 89.20 $525.20
   8 chairs @ 32.50   260.00
                  Total   885.20

   The terms were given on the voucher as 3%, 10 days; net, 30 days. Verify the computations, which may be incorrect, and calculate the correct amount to be paid. If payment is made within the discount period, the amount to be paid is
   A. $761.64
   B. $771.34
   C. $795.20
   D. $858.64
   E. none of the above

   2.____

3. Under the income tax law in effect for last year, an individual who is blind on the last day of the taxable year is entitled to claim an exemption of $600 because of such blindness, in addition to any other exemptions to which he may be entitled.
   Richard Roe, who files his income tax returns on the calendar year basis, became permanently blind on December 15 of last year.
   In filing his income tax return for last year, Mr. Roe may claim an exemption for blindness of
   A. $300
   B. $550
   C. $574
   D. $600
   E. none of the above

   3.____

4. The Jones Company had a merchandise inventory of $24,625 on January 1 of last year. During that year, purchases made by the company amounted to $60,000, sales to $85,065, and cost of goo ds sold to $28,060.
The inventory on December 31 of last year was

    A. $25,065
    B. $28,500
    C. $49,690
    D. $57,005
    E. none of the above

4._____

KEY (CORRECT ANSWERS)

1. D
2. B
3. D
4. E

EXAMINATION SECTION
TEST 1

DIRECTIONS: Each question or incomplete statement is followed by several suggested answers or completions. Select the one that BEST answers the question or completes the statement. *PRINT THE LETTER OF THE CORRECT ANSWER IN THE SPACE AT THE RIGHT.*

1. The independent auditor's PRIMARY objective in reviewing internal control is to provide
    A. assurance of the client's operational efficiency
    B. a basis for reliance on the system and determination of the scope of the auditing procedures
    C. a basis for suggestions for improving the client's accounting system
    D. evidence of the client's adherence to prescribed managerial policies

2. If there is an increase in work-in-process inventory during a period,
    A. cost of goods sold will be greater than cost of goods manufactured
    B. cost of goods manufactured will be greater than cost of goods sold
    C. manufacturing costs (production costs) for the period will be greater than cost of goods manufactured
    D. manufacturing costs for the period will be less than cost of goods manufactured

Questions 3-4.

DIRECTIONS: Questions 3 and 4 are to be answered on the basis of the information given below about the Parr Company and the Farr Company.

The Parr Company purchased 800 of the 1,000 outstanding shares of the Farr Company's common stock for $80,000 on January 1, 2021. During 2021, the Farr Company declared dividends of $8,000 and reported earnings for the year of $20,000.

3. Using the equity method, the investment in Farr Company on the Parr Company's books should show a balance, at December 31, 2021, of
    A. $89,600   B. $$86,400   C. $80,000   D. $73,600

4. If, instead of using the equity method, the Parr Company uses the cost method, the balance, at December 31, 2021, in the investment account, should be
    A. $96,000   B. $86,400   C. $80,000   D. $73,600

Questions 5-6.

DIRECTIONS: Questions 5 and 6 are to be answered on the basis of the information given below about the Fame Corporation.

The Fame Corporation has 50,000 shares of $10 par value common stock authorized, issued, and outstanding. The 50,000 shares were issued at $12 per share. The retained earnings of the company are $60,000.

5. Assuming that the Fame Corporation reacquired 1,000 of its common shares at $15 per share and the par value method of accounting for treasury stock was used, the result would be that
   A. stockholders' equity would increase by $15,000
   B. capital in excess of par would decrease by at least $2,000
   C. retained earnings would decrease by $5,000
   D. common stock would decrease by at least $15,000

6. Assuming that the Fame Corporation reissued 1,000 of its common shares at $11 per share and the cost method of accounting for treasury stock was used, the result would be that
   A. book value per share of common stock would decrease
   B. retained earnings would decrease by $11,000
   C. donated surplus would be credited for $5,500
   D. a gain on reissue of treasury stock account would be charged

7. On January 31, 2012, when the Montana Corporation's stock was selling at $36 per share, its capital accounts were as follows:

Capital Stock (par value $20; 100,000 shares issued)	$2,000,000
Premium on Capital Stock	800,000
Retained Earnings	4,550,000

   If the corporation declares a 100% stock dividend and the par value per share remains at $20, the value of the capital stock would
   A. remain the same
   B. increase to $5,600,000
   C. increase to $5,000,000
   D. decrease

8. In a conventional form of the statement of sources and application of funds, which one of the following would NOT be included?
   A. Periodic amortization of premium of bonds payable
   B. Machinery, fully depreciated and scrapped
   C. Patents written off
   D. Treasury stock purchased from a stockholder

Questions 9-11.

DIRECTIONS: Questions 9 through 11 are to be answered on the basis of the balance sheet shown below for the Argo, Baron and Schooster partnership.

Cash	$ 20,000
Other assets	180,000
Total	$200,000
Liabilities	$50,000
Argo Capital (40%)	37,000
Baron Capital (40%)	65,000
Schooster Capital (20%)	48,000
Total	$200,000

9. If George is to be admitted as a new 1/6 partner without recording goodwill or bonus, George should contribute cash of
   A. $40,000   B. $36,000   C. $33,333   D. $30,000

10. Assume that Schooster is paid $51,000 by George for his interest in the partnership.
    Which of the following choices shows the CORRECT revised capital account for each partner?
    A. Argo, $38,500; Baron, $66,500; George, $51,000
    B. Argo, $38,500; Baron, $66,500; George, $48,000
    C. Argo, $37,000; Baron, $65,000; George, $51,000
    D. Argo, $37,000; Baron, $65,000; George, $48,000

11. Assume that George had not been admitted as a partner but that the partnership was dissolved and liquidated on the basis of the original balance sheet. Non-cash assets with a book value of $90,000 were sold for $50,000 cash. After payment of creditors, all available cash was distributed.
    Which of the following choices MOST NEARLY shows what each of the partners would receive?
    A. Argo, $0; Baron, $13,333; Schooster, $6,667
    B. Argo, $0; Baron, $3,000; Schooster, $17,000
    C. Argo, $6,667; Baron, $6,667; Schooster, $6,666
    D. Argo, $8,000; Baron, $8,000; Schooster, $4,000

12. Which one of the following should be restricted to ONLY one employee in order to assure proper control of assets?
    A. Access to safe deposit box
    B. Placing orders and maintaining relationship with a principal vendor
    C. Collection of a particular past due account
    D. Custody of the petty cash fund

13. To assure proper internal control, the quantities of materials ordered may be omitted from that copy of the purchase order which is
    A. sent to the accounting department
    B. retained in the purchasing department
    C. sent to the party requisitioning the material
    D. sent to the receiving department

14. The Amey Corporation has an inventory of raw materials and parts made up of many different items which are of small value individually but of significant total value
    A BASIC control requirement in such a situation is that
    A. perpetual inventory records should be maintained for all items
    B. physical inventories should be taken on a cyclical basis rather than at year end
    C. storekeeping, production, and inventory record-keeping functions should be separated
    D. requisitions for materials should be approved by a corporate officer

15. In conducting an audit of plant assets, which of the following accounts MUST be examined in order to ascertain that additions to plant assets have been correctly stated and reflect charges that are properly capitalized?
    A. Accounts Receivable
    B. Sales Income
    C. Maintenance and Repairs
    D. Investments

16. Which one of the following is a control procedure that would prevent a vendor's invoice from being paid twice (once upon the original invoice and once upon the monthly statement?
    A. Attaching the receiving report to the disbursement support papers
    B. Prenumbering of disbursement vouchers
    C. Using a limit of reasonable test
    D. Prenumbering of receiving reports

17. A "cut-off" bank statement is received for the period December 1 to December 10, 2021. Very few of the checks listed on the November 30, 2021 bank reconciliation cleared during the cut-off period.
    Of the following, the MOST likely reason for this is
    A. kiting
    B. using certified checks rather than ordinary checks
    C. holding the cash disbursement book open after year end
    D. overstating year-end bank balance

18. "Lapping" is a common type of defalcation.
    Of the audit techniques listed below, the one MOST effective in the detection of "lapping" is
    A. reconciliation of year-end bank statements
    B. review of duplicate deposit slips
    C. securing confirmations from banks
    D. checking footings in cash journals

19. Of the following, the MOST common argument against the use of the negative accounts receivable confirmation is that
    A. cost per response is excessively high
    B. statistical sampling techniques cannot be applied to selection of the sample
    C. client's customers may assume that the confirmation is a request for payment
    D. lack of response does not necessarily indicate agreement with the balance

Questions 20-21.

DIRECTIONS: Questions 20 and 21 are to be answered on the basis of the information in the Payroll Summary given below. This Payroll Summary represents payroll for a monthly period for a particular agency.

		PAYROLL SUMMARY				
			Deductions			
Employee	Total Earnings	FICA	Withhold Tax	State Tax	Other	Net Pay
W	450.00	26.00	67.00	18.00	6.00	333.00
X	235.00	14.00	33.00	8.00	2.00	178.00
Y	341.00	20.00	52.00	14.00	5.00	250.00
Z	275.00	16.00	30.00	6.00	2.40	220.60
Totals	1,301.00	76.00	182.00	46.00	15.40	981.60

20. Based on the data given above, the amount of cash that would have to be available to pay the employees on payday is
    A. $1,301.00   B. $981.60   C. $905.60   D. $662.60

21. Based on the data given above, the amount of cash that would have to be governmental depository is
    A. $334.00   B. $182.00   C. $158.00   D. $76.00

Questions 22-23.

DIRECTIONS: Questions 22 and 23 are to be answered on the basis of the information given below concerning an imprest fund.

Assume a $1,020 imprest fund for cash expenditures is maintained in your agency. As an audit procedure, the fund is counted and the following information results from that count.

Unreimbursed bills properly authorized	$ 345.00
Check from employee T. Jones	125.00
Check from Supervisor R. Riggles	250.00
I.O.U. signed by employee J. Sloan	100.00
Cash counted—coins and bills	200.00
TOTAL	$1,020.00

22. A PROPER statement of cash on hand based upon the data shown above should show a balance of 22.____
   A. $1,020   B. $1,000   C. $545   D. $200

23. Based upon the data shown above, the account reflects IMPROPER handling of the fund because 23.____
   A. vouchers are unreimbursed
   B. the cash balance is too low
   C. employees have used it for loans and check-cashing purposes
   D. the unreimbursed bills should not have been authorized

Question 24-25.

DIRECTIONS: Questions 24 and 25 are to be answered on the basis of the following information.

The following information was taken from the ledgers of the Past Present Corporation:

Common stock had been issued for $6,000,000. This represents 400,000 shares of stock at a stated value of $5 per share. Fifty-thousand shares are in the treasury. These 50,000 shares were acquired for $25 per share. The total undistributed net income since the origin of the corporation was $3,750,000 as of December 31, 2021. Ten-thousand of the treasury stock shares were sold in January 2022 for $30 per share.

24. Based only on the information given above, the TOTAL stockholders' equity that should have been shown on the balance sheet as of December 31,2021 was 24.____
   A. $2,000,000   B. $6,000,000   C. $8,500,000   D. $9,750,000

25. Based only on the information given above, the Retained Earnings as of December 31, 2022 will be 25.____
   A. $2,000,000   B. $3,750,000   C. $3,800,000   D. $4,050,000

Questions 26-29.

DIRECTIONS: Questions 26 through 29 are to be answered on the basis of the following information.

A statement of income for the Dartmouth Corporation for the 2022 fiscal year follows:
Sales $89,000
Cost of Goods Sold   20,000
Gross Margin $34,000
Expenses   20,000
Net Income Before Income Taxes $14,000
Provision for Income Taxes (50%)   7,000
Net Income $7,000

The following errors were discovered relating to the 2022 fiscal year:
- Closing inventory was overstated by $2,100
- A $3,000 expenditure was capitalized during fiscal year 2022 that should have been listed under Expenses. This was subject to 10% amortization taken for a full year
- Sales included $3,500 of deposits received from customers for future orders.
- Accrued salaries of $850 were not included in Cost of Goods Sold
- Interest receivable of $500 was omitted

Assume that the books were not closed and that you have prepared a corrected income statement. Answer Questions 26 through 29 on the basis of your corrected income statement.

26. The gross margin after accounting for adjustments SHOULD BE
    A. $37,500   B. $35,400   C. $31,900   D. $27,550

27. The adjusted income before income taxes SHOULD BE
    A. $5,350   B. $9,550   C. $15,000   D. $15,850

28. The adjusted income after provision for a 50% tax rate SHOULD BE
    A. $7,925   B. $7,500   C. $4,500   D. $2,675

29. After making adjustments, sales to be reported for fiscal year 2022 SHOULD BE
    A. unchanged
    B. increased by $3,500
    C. decreased by $3,500
    D. reduced by $2,100

Questions 30-33.

DIRECTIONS: Questions 30 through 33 are to be answered on the basis of the following budget for the Utility Corporation for 2022.

```
Sales                $550,000
Cost of Goods Sold    320,000
Selling Expenses       75,000
General Expenses       60,000
Net Income             95,000
```

30. If sales are actually 12% above the budget, then ACTUAL sales will be
    A. $550,000   B. $562,000   C. $605,000   D. $616,000

31. If actual costs of goods sold exceed the budget by 10%, then the cost of goods sold will be
    A. $294,400   B. $320,000   C. $605,000   D. $352,000

32. If selling expenses exceed the budget by 10%, the INCREASE in the selling expenses will be
    A. $750   B. $3,750   C. $7,500   D. $8,333

33. If general expenses are under budget by 5%, they will amount to 33._____
    A. $3,000   B. $57,000   C. $60,000   D. $63,000

Questions 34-35.

DIRECTIONS: Questions 34 and 35 are to be answered on the basis of the following information.

    The Yontiff Company began business on January 2, 2021. During the first month, credit sales totaled $100,000. During February, credit sales totaled $125,000. 70% of credit sales are paid during the month of sale, and the balance is collected during the following month.

34. During the month of January, cash collections on credit sales totaled 34._____
    A. $70,000   B. $95,000   C. $100,000   D. $125,000

35. During the month of February, cash collections on credit sales totaled 35._____
    A. $70,000   B. $87,500   C. $117,505   D. $125,000

Questions 36-38.

DIRECTIONS: Questions 36 through 38 are to be answered on the basis of the following information taken from the balance sheet of the F Corporation.

    Common Stock $200 Par $1,400,000
    Premium on Common Stock   115,000
    Deficit   50,000

36. The number of shares of common stock outstanding is 36._____
    A. 200   B. 700   C. 7,000   D. 14,000

37. The total equity is 37._____
    A. $50,000   B. $115,000   C. $1,400,000   D. $1,465,000

38. The book value per share of stock is MOST NEARLY 38._____
    A. $160   B. $200   C. $209   D. $312

Questions 39-40.

DIRECTIONS: Questions 39 and 40 are to be answered on the basis of the following statement.

    You are examining the expense accounts of a contractor and you discover that, although his payroll records show proper deductions from employees, he has never provided for the payroll tax expenses for these employees.

39. As a result of the oversight described in the above statement, the Costs of 39._____
    Construction in Progress as given on the balance sheet will be _____ on the
    balance sheet.
    A. understated   B. overstated   C. unaffected   D. omitted

40. As a result of the oversight described in the above statement, the balance sheet for the firm will reflect an
    A. overstatement of liabilities
    B. understatement of liabilities
    C. overstatement of assets
    D. understatement of assets

40._____

KEY (CORRECT ANSWERS)

1. B	11. D	21. A	31. D
2. C	12. D	22. D	32. C
3. A	13. D	23. C	33. B
4. C	14. C	24. C	34. A
5. B	15. C	25. B	35. C
6. A	16. A	26. D	36. C
7. A	17. C	27. A	37. D
8. B	18. B	28. D	38. C
9. D	19. D	29. C	39. A
10. D	20. B	30. D	40. B

TEST 2

DIRECTIONS: Each question or incomplete statement is followed by several suggested answers or completions. Select the one that BEST answers the question or completes the statement. *PRINT THE LETTER OF THE CORRECT ANSWER IN THE SPACE AT THE RIGHT.*

Questions 1-4.

DIRECTIONS: Questions 1 through 4 are to be answered on the basis of the following information.

In the audit of the Audell Co. for the calendar year 2021, the accountant noted the following errors.

- An adjusting entry for $10 for interest accrued on a customer's $4,000, 60-day, 6% note was not recorded at the end of December 2020. In 2021, the total interest received was credited to interest income.
- Equipment was leased on December 31, 2020 and rental of $300 was paid in advance for the next three months and charged to Rent Expense.
- On November 1, 2020, space was rented at $75 per month. The tenant paid six months rent in advance which was credited to Rent Income.
- Salary expenses in the amount of $60 were not recorded at the end of 2020
- Depreciation in the amount of $80 was not recorded at the end of 2020.
- An error of $200 in addition on the year-end 2020 physical inventory sheets was made. The inventory was overstated.

1. The amount of the net adjustment to Net Income for 2020 is   1._____
   A. Credit $430   B. Debit $430   C. Credit $600   D. Credit $560

2. The net change in asset values at December 31, 2020 is   2._____
   A. Credit $70   B. Debit $70   C. Debit $110   D. Credit $60

3. The net change in liabilities at December 31, 2020 is   3._____
   A. Debit $360   B. Credit $430   C. Debit $560   D. Credit $360

4. The net change in Owner's Equity at December 31, 2020 is   4._____
   A. Debit $720   B. Debit $430   C. Credit $320   D. Credit $720

5. As of October 2, 2021, the Mallory Company's books reflect a balance of $2,104.75 in its account entitled Cash in Bank. A comparison of the book entries with the bank statement showed the following: 5._____
   - A check in the amount of $76.25 outstanding at the end of September 2021 had not been returned.
   - One check, which was returned with the October bank statement, in the amount of $247 had been recorded in the October cash book as $274.
   - A total of $139 of checks issued in October had not been returned with the October bank statement.
   - A deposit of $65 was returned by the bank because of insufficient funds.

- The bank charged a service charge of $3.25 for the month of October which as not reported on the books until November.
- The bank had credited $247 representing a note collected in the amount of $250 which was not picked up on the books until November.
- A deposit of $305.50 was recorded on the books in October but not on the bank statement.

The balance in the bank as shown on the bank statement at October 31, 2021 is
   A. $2,220.25   B. $2,104.75   C. $2,006.25   D. $2,315.25

Questions 6-8.

DIRECTIONS: Questions 6 through 8 are to be answered on the basis of the following information.

A company purchased three cars at $3,150 each on April 2, 2021. Depreciation is to be computed on a mileage basis. The estimated mileage to be considered is 50,000 miles, with a trade-in value of $650 for each car.

After having been driven 8,400 miles, car #1 was completely destroyed on November 23, 2020 and not replaced. The insurance company paid $2,500 for the loss.

As of December 31, 2020, of the two remaining cars, car #2 had been driven 10,300 miles and car #3 was driven 11,500 miles.

On July 10, 2021, after having been driven a total of 24,600 miles, car #2 was sold for $1,800.

Car #3, after having been driven a total of 27,800 miles, was traded in on December 28, 2021 for a new car (#4) that had a list price of $3,000. On the purchase of car #4, the dealer allowed a trade-in value of $1,850.

6. The balance in the Allowance for Depreciation account at December 31, 2020 is   6.____
    A. $1,850   B. $910   C. $1,090   D. $1,110

7. The depreciation expense for the calendar year 2021 is   7.____
    A. $1,530   B. $2,000   C. $2,500   D. $3,00

8. The book value of the new car (car #4) using the income tax method is   8.____
    A. $1,850   B. $3,000   C. $2,500   D. $2,910

Questions 9-10.

DIRECTIONS: Questions 9 and 10 are to be answered on the basis of the following information.

The Pneumatic Corp. showed the following balance sheets at December 31, 2020 and December 31, 2021

	12/31/2020	12/31/2021
Cash	$6,700	$9,000
Accounts Receivable	12,000	11,500
Merchandise Inventory	31,500	32,000
Prepaid Expenses	800	1,000
Equipment	21,000	28,000
	$72,000	$81,500
Accumulated Depreciation	$4,000	$5,500
Accounts Payable	17,500	11,500
Common Stock - $5 Per Share	10,000	5,000
Premium on Common Stock	40,000	50,000
Retained Earnings	10,500	13,000
	$72,000	$81,500

Additional Information:
A further examination of the Pneumatic Corp.'s transactions for 2021 showed the following:
- Depreciation on equipment, $2,500]
- Fully depreciated equipment that cost $1,000 was scrapped, and cost and related accumulated depreciation eliminated.
- Two thousand shares of common stock were sold at $6 per share.
- A cash dividend of $10,000 was paid.

9. A statement of funds provided and applied for the calendar year 2021 would show that net income provided funds in the amount of
    A. $2,500   B. $9,500   C. $15,000   D. $22,500

10. The funds applied to the acquisition of equipment during the calendar year 2021 amounts to
    A. $21,000   B. $28,000   C. $1,000   D. $8,000

11. A company's Wage Expense account had a $19,100 debit balance before any adjustment at the end of its December 31, 2020 fiscal year. The company employs five individuals who earn $15 per day and were paid on Friday for the five days ending on Friday, December 25, 2020. All employees worked during the week ending January 2, 2021.
    The adjusted balance in the Wage Expense account at December 31, 2020 is
    A. $22,300   B. $19,100   C. $19,250   D. $19,325

Questions 12-13.

DIRECTIONS: Questions 12 and 13 are to be answered on the basis of the following information.

The Peach Corp.'s books reflect an account entitled "Allowance for Bad Debts" showing a credit balance of $1,510 as of January 1, 2020.

During 2020, it wrote off 735 of bad debts and increased the allowance for bad debts by an amount equal to ¼ of 1% of sales of $408,000.

During 2021, it wrote off $605 as bad debts and recorded $50 of a debt that had been previously written off.

An addition to the "Allowance for Bad Debts" was provided based upon ¼ of 1% on $478,000 of sales.

12. The balance in the "Allowance for Bad Debts" account at December 31, 2021 is   12._____
 A. $2,550 B. $2,434 C. $2,360 D. $2,240

13. The amount of the Bad Debt expense for the calendar year 2021 is   13._____
 A. $1,195 B. $1,405 C. $2,000 D. $1,510

14. The following ratio is based upon the 2021 financial statements of the Chino Corp.:   14._____
 Number of Times Bond Interest Earned: $28,000/$3,000 = 9.33 times
 Information relating to the corrections of the income data for 2021 follows:
 - Rental payment for December 2021 at $2,00 per month had been recorded in January 2022. No provision has been made for this expense on the 2021 books.
 - During 2021, merchandise shipped on consignment and unsold had been recorded as
   Debit – Accounts Receivable $4,000
   Credit – Sales   4,000
 (Note: The inventory of this merchandise was properly recorded.)
 If the described ratio, Number of Times Bond Interest Earned, was recomputed, taking into consideration the corrections listed above and ignoring tax factors in the calculations, the recomputed Number of Times Bond Interest Earned would be _____ times.
 A. 8.10 B. 7.60 C. 6.20 D. 5.10

Questions 15-16.

DIRECTIONS: Questions 15 and 16 are to be answered on the basis of the following information.

The Delancey Department Store, Inc. sells merchandise on the installment basis. The selling price of its merchandise is $500 and its cost is $325.

At the end of its fiscal year, an examination of its accounts showed the following:
 Sales (Installment $500,000
 Installment Accounts Receivable 280,000
 Sales Commissions   15,000
 Other Expenses   32,000

15. The net income for the fiscal year, before taxes, using the installment method of reporting income, is 15._____
    A. $30,000 B. $20,000 C. $15,000 D. $35,000

16. The balance in the Deferred Income Account at the end of the fiscal year is 16._____
    A. $110,000 B. $80,000 C. $76,000 D. $98,000

Questions 17-18.

DIRECTIONS: Questions 17 and 18 are to be answered on the basis of the following information.

The Merrimac Company sold 8,800 units of a product at $5 per unit during the calendar year 2021. In addition, it has the following transactions:

	Units	Unit Cost
Inventory – January 1, 2021	1,000	$2.80
Purchases – March	1,000	3.00
June	4,000	3.20
September	3,000	3.30
October	1,000	3.50

17. If we assume that selling and administrative expenses cost $8,800, the Net Income for the calendar year 2021, using the first-in first-out method of costing inventory is 17._____
    A. $8,460 B. $7,360 C. $6,600 D. $4,070

18. If we assume that selling and administrative expenses cost $8,800, the Net Income for the calendar year 2021, using the last-in first-out method of costing inventory, is 18._____
    A. $4,550 B. $7,360 C. $6,600 D. $5,000

19. L. Eron and A. Pilott are partners who share income and losses in the ratio 3:2, respectively. The balance in the Profit and Loss account on December 31, 2021, prior to distribution to the partners, is $20,800. Before distributing any profits to the partnership in the agreed ratio, L. Eron is to be given credit for interest on his loan of $60,000, outstanding for the entire year, at 6% per annum. A. Pilott is to receive a bonus of 10% of the net income over $5,100, after deducting the bonus to himself and the interest to L. Eron.
    Giving consideration to all the above information, the total amount of net income to be credited to A. Pilott is 19._____
    A. $8,320 B. $2,080 C. $7,540 D. $15,700

Questions 20-21.

DIRECTIONS: Questions 20 and 21 are to be answered on the basis of the following information.

Schneider and Samuels are partners with capital balances on December 31, 2021 of $15,000 and $25,000, respectively. They share profits in a ratio of 2:1.

Goroff is to be admitted to the partnership. He agrees to be admitted as a partner with a cash investment to give him a one-third interest in the capital and profits of the business. All the parties agree that the goodwill to be granted to Goroff should be valued at $6,000.

20. The required cash to cover Goroff's investment in a business partnership according to the terms stated is
    A. $20,000　　B. $14,000　　C. $6,000　　D. $25,000

21. After his cash investment, and all other initial entries, the credit to Goroff's Capital account is
    A. $20,000　　B. $14,000　　C. $6,000　　D. $25,000

22. The Marlin Corp. sold 7,800 units of its product at $25 per unit and suffered a net loss for its calendar year ending December 31, 2021 of $2,000. The fixed expenses amounted to $80,000 and the variable expenses $117,000. The Marlin Corp. believes that by expending $20,000 in an advertising campaign, it could increase its sales, retaining the $25 per unit selling price, to generate a profit.
Assuming the above facts, the sales revenue for 2021 reflecting the break-even point is
    A. $195,000　　B. $217,000　　C. $250,000　　D. $300,000

23. The Anide Corp., which keeps its books on the accrual basis, had the following transactions for its calendar year ending December 31, 2021.
    - April 15, 2021 – Authorized the issuance of $3,000,000 of 5.5%, 20 year bonds, dated May 1, 2021. Interest to be paid November 1 and May 1.
    - June 1, 2021 – Sold the entire issue at $2,965,150 plus accrued interest
    - November 1, 2021 – Paid the interest due.
    The interest expense for the calendar year 2021 is
    A. $85,000　　B. $165,000　　C. $110,000　　D. $97,300

Questions 24-26.

DIRECTIONS:　Questions 24 through 26 are to be answered on the basis of the following information.

The following information was taken from a worksheet that was used in the preparation of the balance sheet and the profit and loss statement of the Hott Company for 2021.

7 (#2)

The Balance Sheet Contained	Amount
Travel Expense Unpaid	$995
Legal and Collection Fees – Prepaid in Advance	672
Interest Received in Advance	469

The Profit and Loss Statement Contained	Amount
Travel Expenses	$7,343
Legal and Collection Fees	5,461
Interest Income	3,114

    The proper adjusting and closing entries were made on the books of the company by the accountant and the described information was reported on the financial statements. The books are kept on an accrual basis.

    On the basis of the above facts, the balance in each of the following accounts in the trial balance, before adjusting and closing entries were made, was as follows:

24. Travel Expense Account
    A. $8,338   B. $7,343   C. $6,348   D. $995   24.____

25. Legal and Collection Fees Account
    A. $672   B. $4,789   C. $5,461   D. $6,133   25.____

26. Interest Income Account
    A. $3,583   B. $3,114   C. $2,645   D. $469   26.____

Questions 27-28.

DIRECTIONS: Questions 27 and 28 are to be answered on the basis of the following information

The following is the stockholder's equity section of a corporation:

Preferred Stock (7%, cumulative, non-participating, $100 par value, 5,000 shares issued and outstanding)	$500.000
Common Stock ($1.00 par value, 500,000, issued and outstanding)	500,000
	$1,000,000
Deficit	(40,000)
	$960,000

27. Assuming two years' dividends in arrears on the preferred stock, the book value per share of common stock is   27.____
    A. 78¢   B. 80¢   C. 63¢   D. 94¢

28. Assuming two years' dividends in arrears on the preferred stock, the book value per share of preferred stock is   28.____
    A. $130   B. $114   C. $98   D. $140

Questions 29-30.

DIRECTIONS: Questions 29 and 30 are to be answered on the basis of the following information.

Regina Corporation on December 31, 2021 had the following stockholder's equity:

Common Stock ($10 par value), 10,000 shares authorized and outstanding)	$100,000
Retained Earnings	20,000
	$120,000

On December 31, 2021, the Astro Corp. purchased 9,000 shares of the Regina Corporation's outstanding shares, paying $14 per share

29. The entry to eliminate Astro Corp.'s investment and the Regina Corporation's stockholder's equity on consolidation would show a debit or credit to an account called "Excess of Cost Over Book Value" of
   A. Credit, $18,000
   B. Debit, $18,000
   C. Debit, $15,000
   D. Debit, $19,000

29.____

30. If the Regina Corporation had earnings for the calendar year 2021 of $10,000 and had paid out $8,000 of these earnings as dividends, and an entry to eliminate the Astro Corp.'s investment and the Regina Corporation's stockholder's equity were made, the minority stockholder's equity would be
   A. $15,000   B. $10,100   C. $12,200   D. $14,800

30.____

KEY (CORRECT ANSWERS)

1.	B	11.	D	21.	A
2.	A	12.	B	22.	C
3.	D	13.	A	23.	D
4.	B	14.	B	24.	C
5.	A	15.	A	25.	D
6.	C	16.	D	26.	A
7.	A	17.	B	27.	A
8.	D	18.	C	28.	B
9.	C	19.	C	29.	B
10.	D	20.	B	30.	C

TEST 3

DIRECTIONS: Each question or incomplete statement is followed by several suggested answers or completions. Select the one that BEST answers the question or completes the statement. *PRINT THE LETTER OF THE CORRECT ANSWER IN THE SPACE AT THE RIGHT.*

1. For the measurement of net income to be as realistic as possible, it is DESIRABLE that revenue be recognized at the point that
    A. cash is collected from customers
    B. an order for merchandise or services is received from a customer
    C. a deposit or advance payment is received from a customer
    D. goods are delivered or services are rendered to customers

    1.____

2. An accounting principle must receive substantial authoritative support to qualify as "generally accepted."
   Many organizations and agencies have been influential in the development of generally accepted accounting principles, but the MOST influential leadership has come from the
    A. New York Stock Exchange
    B. American Institute of Certified Public Accountants
    C. Securities and Exchange Commission
    D. American Accounting Association

    2.____

3. In which one of the following ways does the declaration and payment of a cash dividend affect corporate net income? It _____ net income.
    A. does not affect   B. reduces
    C. increases   D. capitalizes

    3.____

4. Under which one of the following headings of the corporate balance sheet should the liability for a dividend payable in stock appear?
    A. Current Liabilities   B. Long Term Liabilities
    C. Stockholders' Equity   D. Current Assets

    4.____

5. In which one of the following is "Working Capital" MOST likely to be found?
    A. Income Statement
    B. Analysis of Retained Earnings
    C. Computation of Cost of Capital
    D. Statement of Funds Provided and Applied

    5.____

6. Which one of the following procedures is NOT generally mandatory in auditing a merchandising corporation?
    A. Physical observation of inventory count
    B. Written circularization of accounts receivable
    C. Confirmation of bank balance
    D. Circularization of the stockholders

    6.____

32

7. A company purchased office supplies during 2021 in the total amount of $1,400 and charged the entire amount to the asset account. An inventory of supplies taken on December 31, 2021 shows the cost of unused supplies to be $250. The entry to record this fact, assuming the books have not been closed, involves
   A. credit to capital
   B. debit to supplies Expense
   C. credit to supplies expense
   D. debit to supplies on hand

7.____

8. A corporation's records show $600,000 (credit) in net sales, $200,000 (debit) in year-end accounts receivable, and $2,000 (debit) in Allowance for Bad Debts. The company's aged schedule of accounts receivable indicates a probable future loss from failure to collect year-end receivables in the amount of $6,000.
   Of the following, the MOST correct entry to adjust the Allowance for Bad Debts at year-end is
   A. $1,000 credit
   B. $4,000 credit
   C. $8,000 debit
   D. $8,000 credit

8.____

Questions 9-10.

DIRECTIONS: Questions 9 and 10 are to be answered on the basis of the following information.

A company commenced business in 2021 and purchased inventory as follows:

March	100 units @	$5	$500
June	300	6	1,800
October	200	7	1,400
November	500	6	3,500
December	100	6	600
TOTAL	1,200		$7,800

**Units sold in 2021 amounted to 1,200

9. Under the LIFO inventory principle, the value of the remaining inventory is
   A. $1,700   B. $1,875   C. $2,145   D. $2,225

9.____

10. Under the FIFO inventory principle, the value of the remaining inventory is
    A. $1,650   B. $1,875   C. $2,000   D. $2,025

10.____

11. When doing a trial balance, assume that, as a result of a single error, the total of the credit balances is greater than the total of the debit balances. Which one of the following single errors could NOT be the cause of this discrepancy?
    A. Failure to post a debit
    B. Posting a debit as a credit
    C. Failure to post a credit
    D. Posting a credit twice

11.____

Questions 12-13.

DIRECTIONS: Questions 12 and 13 are to be answered on the basis of the following information.

A and B are partners with capital balances of $20,000 and $30,000, respectively, at June 30, 2021, who share profits and losses, 40% and 60%, respectively. On July 1, 2021, C is to be admitted into the partnership under the following conditions:
- Partnership assets are to be revalued and increased by $10,000
- C is to invest $40,000 but be credited for $30,000 while the remaining $10,000 is to be credited to A and B to compensate them for their pre-existing goodwill.

12. After C is admitted and the proper entries are made, A's capital account will have a credit balance of
    A. $24,500   B. $28,000   C. $30,200   D. $36,000

13. After the admission of C to the partnership, C's share of profits and losses is agreed upon at 20%.
    Assuming no other adjustments, the new percentage for profit and loss distribution to A will be
    A. 18%   B. 32%   C. 36%   D. 45%

14. A company reports as income for tax purposes $70,000 and its book income before the provision for income taxes is $100,000.
    Assuming a 50% tax rate, the PROPER tax expense to be recorded following tax allocation procedures is
    A. $33,000   B. $40,000   C. $50,000   D. $60,000

15. The relationship between the total of cash and current receivables to total current liabilities is commonly referred to by accountants as the
    A. acid-test ratio   B. cross-statement ratio
    C. current ratio   D. R.O.I. ratio

16. On a statement of sources and application of funds, the depreciation expense is normally shown as a(n)
    A. addition to operating income   B. subtraction from funds provided
    C. addition to funds applied   D. reduction from operating income

17. Company A owns 100% of the capital stock of Company B and reports on a consolidated basis. During the year, Company A sold inventory to Company B at a profit of $100,000. One-half of this inventory has been sold at year-end by Company B to the public.
    Which one of the following would be the MOST correct adjustment, if any, to make the consolidated retained earnings conform to generally accepted accounting principles?
    A. Decrease by $50,000   B. Increase by $50,000
    C. Increase by $100,000   D. No adjustment

18. X, Y, and Z are partners with capital of $11,000, $12,000, and $4,500. X has a loan due from the partnership to him of $2,000. Profits and losses are shared in the ratio of 4:5:1, respectively. The partnership has paid off all outside liabilities, and its remaining assets consist of $9,000 in cash and $20,500 of accounts receivable. The partners agree to disburse the $9,000 to themselves in such a way that, even if one of the receivables is realized, no partner will have been overpaid.
Under these conditions, which of the following MOST NEARLY represents the amount to be paid to partner X?
   A. $1,960   B. $3,200   C. $4,800   D. $5,000

18.____

19. R Company needs $2,000,000 to finance an expansion of plant facilities. The company expects to earn a return of 15% on this investment before considering the cost of capital or income taxes. The average income tax rate for the R Company is 40%.
If the company raises the funds by issuing 6% bonds at face value, the earnings available to common stockholders after the new plant facilities are in operation may be expected to increase by
   A. $65,000   B. $70,000   C. $108,000   D. $116,000

19.____

20. The budget for a given factory overhead cost was $150,000 for the year. The actual cost for the year was $125,000.
Based on these facts, it can be said that the plant manager has done a better job than expected in controlling this cost if the cost is a
   A. semi-variable cost
   B. variable cost and actual production was 83 1/3% of budgeted production
   C. semi-variable cost which includes a fixed element of $25,000 per period
   D. variable cost and actual production was equal to budgeted production

20.____

21. The Home Office account on the books of the City Branch shows a credit balance of $15,000 at the end of a year and the City Branch account on the books of the Home Office shows a debit balance of $12,000.
Of the following, the MOST likely reason for the discrepancy in the two accounts is that
   A. merchandise shipped by the Home Office to the branch has not been recorded by the branch
   B. the Home Office has not recorded a branch loss for the first quarter of the year
   C. the branch has just mailed a check for $3,000 to the Home Office which has not yet been received by the Home Office
   D. the Home Office has not yet recorded the branch profit for the first quarter of the year

21.____

22. The concept of matching costs and revenues means that
   A. the expenses offset against revenues should be related to the same time period
   B. revenues are at least as great as expenses on the average
   C. revenues and expenses are equal
   D. net income equals revenues minus expenses for the same earning period

22.____

23. If the inventory at the end of the current year is understated, and the error is not caught during the following year, the effect is to
    A. *overstate* the income for the two-year period
    B. *overstate* income this year and *understate* income next year
    C. *understate* income this year and *overstate* income next year
    D. *understate* income this year, with no effect on the income of the next year

23._____

KEY (CORRECT ANSWERS)

1.	D	11.	C
2.	B	12.	B
3.	A	13.	B
4.	C	14.	C
5.	D	15.	A
6.	D	16.	A
7.	B	17.	A
8.	D	18.	C
9.	A	19.	C
10.	C	20.	D

21. D
22. A
23. C

EXAMINATION SECTION
TEST 1

DIRECTIONS: Each question or incomplete statement is followed by several suggested answers or completions. Select the one that BEST answers the question or completes the statement. *PRINT THE LETTER OF THE CORRECT ANSWER IN THE SPACE AT THE RIGHT.*

1. The Donaldson Company's cash balance includes a sum of $1,200,000 appropriated by the Board of Directors for the purchase of new equipment. On its financial statements, this amount should be included on the
    A. balance sheet as a current asset
    B. balance sheet as a non-current asset, specifically identified
    C. balance sheet as a fixed asset, included as part of plant cost
    D. income statement as a non-operating expense

2. The trial balance of the Davis Corporation as of June 30, 2021, the end of its fiscal year, included opposite the title ESTIMATED FEDERAL INCOME TAXES ACCRUED the amount of $35,000, which included the company's estimate of the Federal income tax it would have to pay for its 2021 fiscal year and the amount of an unpaid additional assessment for the 2018 fiscal year.
    This amount should appear on the balance sheet as a(n)
    A. general reserve
    B. reduction of current assets
    C. current liability
    D. allocation of retained income

3. A weekly payroll check was issued to an hourly employee based upon 88 hours of work instead of the normal 38 hours. The time card was somewhat illegible, and the number looked like it could have been 88.
    The BEST control procedure to prevent such an error would be
    A. desk checking
    B. a hash total
    C. a limit test
    D. a code check

4. In preparing a bank reconciliation, outstanding checks should be
    A. *deducted* from the balance per books
    B. *deducted* from the balance per bank statement
    C. *added* to the balance per books
    D. *added* to the balance per bank statement

5. Independence is essential and is expected under the generally accepted auditing standards.
    The face and appearance of integrity and objectivity are BEST maintained if
    A. the auditor is unbiased
    B. the auditor is aware of the problem of third party liability
    C. there is no financial relationship between the client and the auditor
    D. all financial relationships between the auditor and the client are reported in footnote form

6. An audit program is a plan of action and is used to guide the auditor in planning his work.
   Such a program, if standardized, must be modified to
   A. observe limits that management places on the audit
   B. counteract internal control weaknesses
   C. meet the limited training of the auditor
   D. limit interference with work of the firm being audited

7. In auditing the *Owner's Equity* section of any company, the section related to a publicly-held corporation which uses a transfer agent and registrar would be more intricate than the audit of a partnership.
   Therefore, the procedure that an auditor should use in this case is to
   A. obtain a listing of the number of shares of securities outstanding
   B. make a count of the number of shareholders
   C. determine that all stock transfers have been properly handled
   D. count the number of shares of stock in the treasury

8. In recent years, it has become increasingly more important to determine the correct number of shares outstanding when auditing the owner's equity accounts.
   This is TRUE because
   A. there has been more fraud with respect to securities issued
   B. there are increased complexities determining the earnings per share
   C. there are more large corporations
   D. the auditor has to test the amount of invested capital

9. In auditing corporation records, an auditor must refer to some corporate documents that are not accounting documents.
   The one of the following to which he is LEAST likely to refer is
   A. minutes of the board of directors meeting
   B. articles of incorporation of the corporation
   C. correspondence with public relations firms and the shareholders
   D. the by-laws of the corporation

10. A generally accepted auditing procedure which has been required by AICPA requirements is the observation of inventories.
    Since it is impossible to observe the entire inventory of a large firm, the auditor may satisfy this requirement by
    A. establishing the balance by the use of a gross profit percentage method
    B. using sampling procedures to verify the count made by the client
    C. accepting the perpetual inventory records, once he has established that the entries are arithmetically accurate
    D. accepting the management statement that the inventory is correct as to quantity where observation is difficult

11. Materiality is an important consideration in all aspects of an audit examination. Attention must be given to accounts with small and zero balances when examining accounts payable.
    This does not conflict with the concept of materiality because

A. The size of a balance is no clue to possible understatement of a liability
B. the balance of the account is not a measure of materiality
C. a sampling technique may suggest examining those accounts under consideration
D. the total of the accounts payable may be a material amount and, therefore, no individual account payable should be eliminated from review

12. In establishing the amount of a liability recorded on the books, which of the following types of evidence should an auditor consider to be the MOST reliable?
    A. A check issued by the company and bearing the payee's endorsement which is included with the bank statement
    B. Confirmation of an account payable balance mailed by and returned directly to the auditor
    C. A sales invoice issued by the client with a delivery receipt from an outside trucker attached
    D. A working paper prepared by the client's accountant and reviewed by the client's controller

13. Prior period adjustments as defined by APIB Opinion #9 issued by the AICPA never flow through the income statement.
    The one of the following which is NOT one of the four criteria established b APB #9 for meeting the qualifications for treatment as a prior period adjustment is that the adjustment item
    A. is not susceptible to reasonable extension prior to the current period
    B. must be determined primarily by someone other than company management
    C. can be specifically identified with and directly related to the business activities of a particular prior period
    D. when placed in the current period would give undesirable results of operations

14. The subject caption which does NOT belong in a report of a financial audit and review of operations of public agency is
    A. Audit Program
    B. Description of Agency Organization and Function
    C. Summary Statement of Findings
    D. Details of Findings

15. At the inception of an audit of a public assistance agency, you ascertain that the one-year period of your audit includes 240,000 serially numbered payment vouchers.
    The sample selection which would enable you to render the MOST generally acceptable opinion on the number of ineligible persons receiving public assistance is
    A. the number of vouchers issued in a one-month period
    B. every hundredth voucher
    C. a random statistical selection
    D. an equal size block of vouchers from each month

16. Of the following, the one which BEST describes an internal control system is the
    A. division of the handling and recording of each transaction into component parts so as to involve at least two persons, with each performing an unduplicated part of each transaction
    B. expansion of the worksheet to include provisions for adjustments to the books of account prior to preparation of the financial statements
    C. recording of transactions affecting negotiable instruments in accordance with the principles of debit and credit, and giving these instruments special treatment if they are interest or non-interest bearing notes
    D. taking of discounts, when properly authorized by the vendor, as an incentive for prompt payment

16.____

17. During audits of small businesses, an accountant is less likely to find that these establishments have a system of internal control comparable to larger firms because small businesses GENERALLY
    A. can absorb the cost of small fraudulent acts which may be perpetrated
    B. benefit more than larger firms by prevention of fraud than by detection of fraud
    C. have limited staff and the costs of maintaining the system are high
    D. use a double entry system which serves as a substitute for internal control

17.____

18. In the performance of a financial audit, especially one where there is a need for a thorough knowledge of law, an accountant would BEST be advised to
    A. rely on the testimony of witnesses, as they may be found during the course of the audit, in preference to the written record
    B. rely on the presumption that the client's actions are illegal when the audit discloses meager facts or evidence
    C. be aware of the specific legal objectives he is attempting to attain by means of his audit
    D. be aware of different conclusions he can reach depending upon what facts are stressed or discounted in his audit

18.____

19. There are various types of budgets which are used to measure different government activities.
    The type of budget which PARTICULARLY measures input of resource as compared with output service is the _____ budget.
    A. capital   B. traditional   C. performance   D. program

19.____

20. Bank balances are usually confirmed through the use of a standard bank confirmation form as authorized by the AICPA and the Bank Administration Institute.
    In addition to bank balances, these confirmations ALSO confirm
    A. the credit rating of the client
    B. details of all deposits during the past month
    C. loans and contingent liabilities outstanding
    D. securities held by the bank as custodian or the client

20.____

KEY (CORRECT ANSWERS)

1.	B	11.	A
2.	C	12.	B
3.	C	13.	D
4.	B	14.	A
5.	C	15.	C
6.	B	16.	A
7.	A	17.	C
8.	B	18.	C
9.	C	19.	C
10.	B	20.	C

TEST 2

DIRECTIONS: Each question or incomplete statement is followed by several suggested answers or completions. Select the one that BEST answers the question or completes the statement. *PRINT THE LETTER OF THE CORRECT ANSWER IN THE SPACE AT THE RIGHT.*

Questions 1-3.

DIRECTIONS: Questions 1 through 3 are based on the classification of items into the appropriate section of a corporation balance sheet. The list of sections to be used is given below:

   Current Assets   Investments
   Current Liabilities   Long-term Liabilities
   Deferred Credits   Paid-in Capital
   Deferred Expenses   Plant Assets
   Intangible assets   Retained Earnings

1. With respect to *Bonds Payable Due* in 2021, the PROPER classification is 1.____
   A. Investments   B. Paid-in Capital
   C. Retained Earnings   D. Long-term Liabilities

2. With respect to *Premium on Common Stock*, the PROPER classification is 2.____
   A. Intangible Assets   B. Investments
   C. Retained Earnings   D. Paid-in Capital

3. With respect to *Organization Costs,* the PROPER classification is 3.____
   A. Intangible Assets   B. Investments
   C. Plant Assets   D. Current Liabilities

4. J. Frost operates a small, individually owned repair service and maintains adequate double entry records. A review of his bank accounts and other available financial records yields the following information: 4.____
   Deposits made during 2021 per bank statements totaled $360,000. Deposits included a bank loan of $25,000 and an additional investment by Frost of $5,000. Disbursements during 2021 per bank statements totaled $305,000. This amount includes personal withdrawals of $28,500 and repayment of debt of $15,000.
   The Net Equity of J. Frost at January 1, 2021 was determined to be $61,000. Net Equity of J. Frost at December 31, 2021 was determined to be $67,000. Based upon the *Net Worth* method, Frost's net income for the year ended December 31, 2021 was
   A. $6,000   B. $29,500   C. $41,500   D. $55,000

Questions 5-8.

DIRECTIONS: Questions 5 through 8 are based on the following Balance Sheet, Income statement, and Notes relating to the books and records of the Hartman Corporation.

2 (#2)

BALANCE SHEET (000 omitted)

	September 30, 2020 Debit	September 30, 2020 Credit	September 30, 2021 Debit	September 30, 2021 Credit
Cash	$18		$31	
Accounts Receivable	28		26	
Inventory	10		15	
Land	40		81	
Building and equipment (Net)	60		65	
Accounts Payable		$10		$11
Notes Payable		2		2
Bonds Payable		50		50
Mortgage Payable		20		46
Common Stock		50		86
Retained Earnings		24		23
	$156	$156	$218	$218

INCOME STATEMENT FOR FISCAL YEAR ENDING SEPTEMBER 30, 2021

Income:
 Sales $85
 Cost of Sales 40
 Gross Margin $45

Expenses:
 Depreciation $5
 Loss on Sale of Fixed Assets 2
 Other Operating Expenses 32
 Total Expenses $39
  Net Income $6

NOTES:
1. Dividend declared during the year 2021, $7,000
2. Acquired land; gave $36,000 common stock and cash for the balance.
3. Wrote off $1,000 accounts receivable and as uncollectible.
4. Acquired equipment; gave note secured by mortgage of $26,000.
5. Sold equipment; net cost per books, $16,000, sales price $14,000.

5. The amount of funds provided from net income for the year ended September 30 2021 is   5.____
   A. $6,000   B. $7,000   C. $13,000   D. $14,000

6. Financing and investing activities not affecting working capital are reported under the rules of APB #19. Notes 1 through 5 refer to various transactions on the books of the Hartman Corporation.   6.____
   Select the answer which refers to the numbers reflecting the concept mentioned here.
   A. Notes 1, 3, and 5   B. Notes 2 and 4
   C. Notes 2, 4, and 5   D. All five notes

7. Funds applied for the acquisition of the land are
   A. $5,000   B. $36,000   C. $41,000   D. None

8. The net change in working capital from 2020 to 2021 is
   A. $6,000   B. $16,000   C. $22,000   D. $35,000

9. Sales during July 2021 for the Magnum Corporation, operating in Los Angeles, were $378,000, of which $150,000 were on account. The sales figures given include the total sales tax charged to retail customers. (Assume a sales tax rate on all sales of 8%.)
   The CORRECT sales tax liability for July 2021 should be shown as
   A. $3,024   B. $18,240   C. $28,000   D. $30,240

10. Of the following statement ratios, the one that BEST represents a measure of cost efficiency is
    A. Acid Test Ratio
    B. Operating Costs to Net Sales Ratio
    C. Cost of Manufacturing to Plant Assets Radio
    D. Earnings Per Share

Questions 11-13.

DIRECTIONS: Questions 11 through 13 are to be answered on the basis of the following information:

An examination of the books and records of the Kay May Corporation, a machinery wholesaler, reveals the following facts for the year ended December 31, 2021:

   a. Merchandise was sold and billed F.O.B. shipping point on December 31, 2021 at a sales price of $7,500. Although the merchandise costing $6,000 was ready for shipment on that date, the trucking company did not call for the merchandise until January 2, 2022. It was not included in the inventory count taken on December 31, 2021.
   b. Merchandise with a sales price of $5,500 was billed and shipped to the customer on December 31, 2021. The merchandise costing $4,800 was not included in the inventory count taken on that day. Terms of sale were F.O.B. destination.
   c. Merchandise costing $5,000 was recorded as a purchase on December 26, 2021. The merchandise was not included in the inventory count taken on December 31, 2021 since, upon examination, it was found to be defective and was in the process of being returned to the vendor.
   d. Merchandise costing $2,500 was received on December 31, 2021. It was included in the inventory count on that date. Although the invoice was dated January 3, 2022, the purchase was recorded in the December 2021 Purchases Journal.
   e. Merchandise costing $4,000 was received on January 3, 2022. It was shipped F.O.B. destination, and the invoice was dated December 30, 2021. The invoice was recorded in the December 2021 Purchases Journal, and the merchandise was included in the December 31, 2021 inventory.

11. The net change to correct the inventory value as of December 31, 2021 is: 11.____
    A. Increase $800   B. Increase $5,800
    C. Increase $6,800   D. Decrease $12,055

12. The net change to correct the sales figure for the year 2021 is: 12.____
    A. Increase $2,000   B. Decrease $5,500
    C. Decrease $7,500   D. $13,000

13. The net change to correct the purchases figure for the year 2021 is: 13.____
    A. Decrease $11,500   B. Decrease $4,000
    C. Decrease $5,000   D. Decrease $9,000

Questions 14-18.

DIRECTIONS: Each of the following Questions 14 through 18 consists of a description of a transaction that indicates a two-fold effect on the Balance Sheet. Each of these transactions may be classified under one of the following categories:

A. Assets are Understated, Retained Earnings are Understated
B. Assets are Overstated, Retained Earnings are Overstated
C. Liabilities are Understated, Retained Earnings are Overstated
D. Liabilities are Overstated, Retained Earnings are Understated

Examine each question carefully. In the correspondingly numbered space at the right, print the letter preceding the category above which BEST describes the effect of each transaction on the Balance Sheet as of December 31, 2021.

14. A major equipment purchase was made at the beginning of 2021. The equipment had an estimated six-year useful life, and depreciation was overlooked at December 31, 2021. 14.____

15. Unearned Rental Income was properly credited when received early in the year. No year-end adjustment was made to transfer the earned portion to an appropriate account. 15.____

16. Goods on hand at a branch office were excluded from the year-end physical inventory. The purchase of these goods had been properly recorded 16.____

17. Accrued Interest on Notes Receivable was overlooked as of December 31, 2021. 17.____

18. Accrued Federal Income Taxes for 2021 have never been recorded. 18.____

19. The following are account balances for the dates shown:

	Dec. 31, 2021	Dec. 31, 2020
Current Assets:		
Cash	$168,000	$60,000
Short-term investments	16,000	20,000
Accounts receivable (net)	160,000	100,000
Inventory	60,000	40,000
Prepaid expenses	4,000	40,000
Current Liabilities:		
Accounts payable	110,000	80,000
Dividends payable	30,000	0

Given the above account balances, the CHANGE in working capital is a(n)
A. increase of $128,000
B. decrease of $128,000
C. increase of $188,000
D. decrease of $188,000

19.____

20. In conducting an audit of plant assets, which of the following accounts MUST be examined in order to ascertain that additions to plant assets have been correctly stated and reflect charges that are properly capitalized?
A. Accounts receivable
B. Sales income
C. Maintenance and repairs
D. Investments

20.____

KEY (CORRECT ANSWERS)

1.	D	11.	A
2.	D	12.	B
3.	A	13.	D
4.	B	14.	B
5.	C	15.	D
6.	B	16.	A
7.	A	17.	A
8.	B	18.	C
9.	C	19.	A
10.	B	20.	C

though
ACCOUNTING

EXAMINATION SECTION

TEST 1

DIRECTIONS: Each question or incomplete statement is followed by several suggested answers or completions. Select the one that BEST answers the question or completes the statement. *PRINT THE LETTER OF THE CORRECT ANSWER IN THE SPACE AT THE RIGHT.*

Questions 1-5.

DIRECTIONS: Questions 1 through 5 are to be answered on the basis of the following information.

When balance sheets are analyzed, working capital always receives close attention. Adequate working capital enables a company to carry sufficient inventories, meet current debts, take advantage of cash discounts and extend favorable terms to customers. A company that is deficient in working capital and unable to do these things is in a poor competitive position.

Below is a Trial Balance as of June 30, 2021, in alphabetical order, of the Worth Corporation.

	Debits	Credits
Accounts Payable		$50,000
Accounts Receivable	$40,000	
Accrued Expenses Payable		10,000
Capital Stock		10,000
Cash	20,000	
Depreciation Expense	5,000	
Inventory	60,000	
Plant & Equipment (net)	30,000	
Retained Earnings		20,000
Salary Expense	35,000	
Sales		100,000
	$190,000	$190,000

1. The Worth Corporation's Working Capital, based on the data above, is 1.____
   A. $50,000   B. $55,000   C. $60,000   D. $65,000

2. Which one of the following transactions increases Working Capital? 2.____
   A. Collecting outstanding accounts receivable
   B. Borrowing money from the bank based upon a 90-day interest-bearing note payable
   C. Paying off a 60-day note payable to the bank
   D. Selling merchandise at a profit

3. The Worth Corporation's Current Ratio, based on the above data, is
   A. 1.7 to 1   B. 2 to 1   C. 2.5 to 1   D. 4 to 3

4. Which one of the following transactions decreases the Current Ratio?
   A. Collecting an account receivable
   B. Borrowing money from the bank giving a 90-day interest-bearing note payable
   C. Paying off a 60-day note payable to the bank
   D. Selling merchandise at a profit

5. The payment of a current liability, such as Payroll Taxes Payable, will
   A. *increase* the current ratio but have no effect on the working capital
   B. *increase* the Working Capital, but have no effect on the current ratio
   C. *decrease* both the current ratio and working capital
   D. *increase* both the current ratio and working capital

6. During the year 2021, the Ramp Equipment Co. made sales to customers totaling $100,000 that were subject to sales taxes of $8,000. Net cash collections totaled $92,000. Discounts of $3,000 were allowed. During the year 2021, uncollectible accounts in the sum of $2,000 were written off the books.
   The net change in accounts receivable during the year 2021 was
   A. $10,500   B. $11,000   C. $13,000   D. $13,500

7. The Grable Co. received a $6,000, 8%, 60-day note dated May 1, 2021 from a customer. On May 16, 2021, the Grable Co. discounted the note at 6% at the bank.
   The net proceeds from the discounting of the note amounted to
   A. $5,954.40   B. $6,034.40   C. $6,064.80   D. $6,080.00

8. In reviewing the customers' accounts in the Accounts Receivable Ledger for the entire year 2020, the following errors are discovered.
   - A sale in the amount of $500 to the J. Brown Co. was erroneously posted to the K. Brown Co.
   - A sales return of $100 from the Gale Co. was debited to their account.
   - A check was received from a customer, M. White and Co. in payment of a sale of $500 less 2% discount. The check was entered properly in the cash receipts book but was posted to the M. White and Co. account in the amount of $490.

   The difference between the controlling account and its related accounts receivable schedule amounts to
   A. $90   B. $110   C. $190   D. $210

9. Assume that you are called upon to audit a cash fund. You find in the cash drawer postage stamps and I.O.U.'s signed by employees, totaling together $425.
   In preparing a financial report, the $425 should be reported as
   A. petty cash   B. investments
   C. supplies and receivables   D. cash

10. On December 31, 2020, before adjustment, Accounts Receivable had a debit balance of $60,000 and the Allowance for Uncollectible Accounts had a debit balance of $1,000.
If credit losses are estimated at 5% of Accounts Receivable and the estimated method of reporting bad debts is used, then bad debts expense for the year 2020 would be reported as
A. $1,000   B. $2,000   C. $3,000   D. $4,000

10.____

Questions 11-12.

DIRECTIONS: Questions 11 and 12 are to be answered on the basis of the following information.

Accrued salaries payable on $7,500 had not been recorded on December 31, 2021. Office supplies on hand of $2,500 at December 32, 2021 were erroneously treated as expense instead of inventory. Neither of these errors was discovered or corrected.

11. These two errors would cause the income for 4021 to be
A. *understated* by $5,000   B. *overstated* by $5,000
C. *understated* by $10,000   D. *overstated* by $10,000

11.____

12. The effect of these errors on the retained earnings at December 31, 2021 would be
A. *understated* by $2,500   B. *overstated* by $2,500
C. *understated* by $5,000   D. *overstated* by $5,000

12.____

Questions 13-14.

DIRECTIONS: Questions 13 and 14 are to be answered on the basis of the following information.

Albano, Borrone, and Colluci operate a retail store under the trade name of ABC. Their partnership agreement provides for equaling sharing profits and losses after salaries of $5,000 to Albano, $10,000 to Borrone, and $15,000 to Colluci.

13. If the net income of the partnership (prior to salaries to partners) is $21,000, then Albano's share of the profits, considering all aspects of the agreement, is determined to be
A. $2,000   B. $3,000   C. $5,000   D. $7,000

13.____

14. The share of the profits that apply to Borrone, similarly, is determined to be
A. $2,000   B. $3,000   C. $5,000   D. $7,000

14.____

Questions 15-17.

DIRECTIONS: Questions 15 through 17 are to be answered on the basis of the following information.

4 (#1)

The Kay Company currently uses FIFO for inventory valuation. Their records for the year ended June 30, 2021 reflect the following:

July 1, 2021 inventory 100,000 units @ 7.50
Purchases during year 400,000 units @ $8.00
Sales during year 350,000 units @ $15.00
Expenses exclusive of income taxes $1,290,000
Cash balance on June 30, 2021 $250,000
Income tax rate 34%

Assume the July 1, 2021 inventory will be the LIFO Base Inventory.

15. If the company should change to the LIFO as of June 30, 2021, then their income before taxes for the year-ended June 30, 2021, as compared with the income FIFO method, will be 15.____
 A. *increased* by $50,000
 B. *decreased* by $50,000
 C. *increased* by $100,000
 D. *decreased* by $100,000

16. Assuming the given tax rate (45%), the use of the LIFO method will result in an approximate tax expense for fiscal 2021 of 16.____
 A. $45,000 B. $50,000 C. $72,000 D. $94,500

17. Assuming the given tax rate (45%), the use of the LIFO inventory method compared with the FIFO method, will result in a change in the approximate income tax expense for fiscal year 2021 as follows: 17.____
 A. *Increase* of $22,500
 B. *Decrease* of $22,500
 C. *Increase* of $45,000
 D. *Decrease* of $45,000

18. An accountant in an agency, in addition to his regular duties, has been assigned to train a newly appointed assistant accountant. The latter believes that he is not being given the training that he needs in order to perform his duties. Accordingly, the MOST appropriate FIRST step for the assistant accountant to take in order to secure the needed training is to 18.____
 A. register for the appropriate courses at the local college as soon as possible
 B. advise the accountant in a formal memo that his apparent lack of interest in the training is impeding his progress
 C. discuss the matter with the accountant privately and try to discover what seems to be the problem
 D. secure such training informally from more sympathetic accountants in the agency

19. You have worked very hard and successfully helped complete a difficult audit of a large corporation doing business with your agency. Your supervisor gives you a brief nod of approval when you expected a more substantial degree of recognition. You are angry and feel unappreciated. 19.____

Of the following, the MOST appropriate course of action for you to take would be to
- A. voice your displeasure to your fellow workers at being taken for granted by an unappreciative supervisor
- B. say nothing now and assume that your supervisor's nod of approval may be his customary acknowledgment of efforts well done
- C. let your supervisor know that he owes you something by repeatedly stressing the outstanding job you've done
- D. ease off on your work quality and productivity until your efforts are finally appreciated

20. You have been assisting in an audit of the books and records of businesses as a member of a team. The accountant in charge of your group tells you to start preliminary work independently on a new audit. This audit is to take place at the offices of the business. The business officers have been duly notified of the audit date. Upon arrival at their offices, you find that their records and files are in disarray and that their personnel are antagonistic and uncooperative.
Of the following, the MOST desirable action for you to take is to
- A. advise the business officers that serious consequences may follow unless immediate cooperation is secured
- B. accept whatever may be shown or told you on the grounds that it would be unwise to further antagonize uncooperative personnel
- C. inform your supervisor of the situation and request instructions
- D. leave immediately and return later in the expectation of encountering a more cooperative attitude

KEY (CORRECT ANSWERS)

1.	C	11.	C
2.	D	12.	A
3.	B	13.	A
4.	B	14.	D
5.	A	15.	B
6.	B	16.	C
7.	B	17.	B
8.	D	18.	C
9.	C	19.	B
10.	D	20.	C

TEST 2

DIRECTIONS: Each question or incomplete statement is followed by several suggested answers or completions. Select the one that BEST answers the question or completes the statement. *PRINT THE LETTER OF THE CORRECT ANSWER IN THE SPACE AT THE RIGHT.*

Questions 1-3.

DIRECTIONS: Questions 1 through 3 are to be answered on the basis of the following information.

The city is planning to borrow money with a 5-year, 7% bond issue totaling $10,000,000 on principle when other municipal issues are paying 8%.
Present value of $1 – 8% - 5 years -68057
Present value of annual interest payments – annuity 8% - 5 years – 3.99271

1. The funds obtained from this bond issue (ignoring any costs relating to issuance) would be, approximately, 1.____
   A. $9,515,390   B. $10,000,000   C. $10,484,620   D. $10,800,000

2. At the date of maturity, the bonds will be redeemed at 2.____
   A. $9,515,390   B. $10,000,000   C. $10,484,610   D. $10,800,000

3. As a result of this issue, the ACTUAL interest costs each year as related to the 7% interest payments will 3.____
   A. be the same as paid ($700,000)
   B. be more than $700,000
   C. be less than $700,000
   D. fluctuate depending on the market conditions

4. Following the usual governmental accounting concepts, the activities of a municipal employee retirement plan, which is financed by equal employer and employee contributions, should be accounted for in a(n) 4.____
   A. agency fund   B. intragovernmental service fund
   C. special assessment fund D. trust fund

Questions 5-7.

DIRECTIONS: Questions 5 through 7 are to be answered on the basis of the following information.

The Balance Sheet of the JLA Corp. is as follows:

Current Assets	$50,000	Current Liabilities	$20,000
Other Assets	75,000	Common Stock	75,000
Total	$125,000	Retained Earnings	30,000
		Total	$125,000

52

5. The working capital of the JLA Corp. is
   A. $30,000   B. $50,000   C. $105,000   D. $125,000

6. The operating ratio of the JLA Corp. is
   A. 2 to 1   B. 2½ to 1   C. 1 to 2   D. 1 to 2½

7. The stockholders' equity is
   A. $30,000   B. $75,000   C. $105,000   D. $125,000

8. This question is based on the following figures taken from a set of books for the year ending June 30, 2021.

	Trial Balance Before Adjustments	Trial Balance After Adjustments
Commissions Payable	cr...	cr $1,550
Office Salaries	dr $9,500	dr $10,680
Rental Income	cr $4,300	cr $4,900
Accumulated Depreciation	cr $7,000	cr $9,700
Supplies Expense	dr $1,760	dr $1,200

   As a result of the adjustments reflected in the adjusted trial balance, the net income of the company before taxes will be
   A. *increased* by $4,270   B. *decreased* by $4,270
   C. *increased* by $5,430   D. *decreased* by $5,430

9. This question is based on the following facts concerning the operations of a manufacturer of office desks.

Date	Item	Units	% Complete
Jan. 1, 2021	Goods in Process Inventory	4,260 units	40% complete
Dec. 31, 2021	Goods in Process Inventory	3,776 units	25% complete
Jan. 1, 2021	Finished Goods Inventory	2,630 units	
Dec. 31, 2021	Finished Goods Inventory	3,180 units	

   Sales consummated during the year: 127,460 units

   Assuming that all the desks are the same style, the number of equivalent complete units, manufactured during the year 2021 is
   A. 127,250   B. 127,460   C. 128,010   D. 131,510

Questions 10-11.

DIRECTIONS: Questions 10 and 11 are to be answered on the basis of the following information.

On January 1, 2021, the Lenox Corporation was organized with a cash investment of $50,000 by the shareholders. Some of the corporate records were destroyed. However, you were able to discover the following facts from various sources.

Accounts Payable at December 31, 2021 (arising from merchandise purchased)	$16,000
Accounts Receivable at December 31, 2021 (arising from the sales of merchandise)	$18,000
Sales for the calendar year 2021	$94,000
Inventory, December 31, 2021	20,000
Cost of Goods Sold is 60% of the selling price	
Bank loan outstanding – December 31, 2021	15,000
Expenses paid in cash during the year	35,000
Expenses incurred but unpaid as of December 31, 2021	4,000
Dividend paid	25,000

10. The CORRECT cash balance is 10._____
   A. $5,600   B. $20,600   C. $38,600   D. $40,600

11. The stockholders' equity on December 31, 2021 is 11._____
   A. $23,600   B. Deficit of $26,400
   C. $27,600   D. $42,400

Questions 12-13.

DIRECTIONS: Questions 12 and 13 are to be answered on the basis of the following facts developed from the records of a company that sells its merchandise on the installment plan.

Sales	Calendar Year 2020	Calendar Year 2021
Total volume of sales	$80,000	$100,000
Cost of Goods Sold	60,000	40,000
Gross Profit	$20,000	$60,000
Cash Collections		
From 2020 Sales	$18,000	$36,000
From 2021 Sales		22,000
Total Cash Collections	$18,000	$58,000

12. Using the deferred profit method of determining thee income from installment 12._____
    sales, the gross profit on sales for the calendar year 2020 was
    A. $4,500   B. $18,000   C. $20,000   D. None

13. Using the deferred profit method of determining the income from installment 13._____
    sales, the gross profit on sales for the calendar year 2021 was
    A. $22,000   B. $22,200   C. $60,000   D. None

Questions 14-15.

DIRECTIONS: Questions 14 and 15 are to be answered on the basis of the data developed from an examination of the records of Ralston, Inc. for the month of April 2021.

4 (#2)

Beginning Inventory: 10,000 units @ $4.00 each

	Purchases		Sales
April 10	20,000 units @ $5 each	April 13	15,000 units @ $8 each
17	60,000 units @ $6 each	21	50,000 units @ $9 each
26	40,000 units @ $7 each	27	50,000 units @ $10 each

14. The gross profit on sales for the month of April, 2021, assuming that inventory is priced on the FIFO basis, is   14.____
    A. $330,000   B. $355,000   C. $395,000   D. $435,000

15. The gross profit on sales for the month of April 2021, assuming that inventory is priced on the LIFO basis is   15.____
    A. $330,000   B. $355,000   C. $395,000   D. $435,000

16. This question is to be answered on the basis of the data presented for June 30, 2021.   16.____

Balance per Bank Statement	$24,019.00
Balance per General Ledger	20,592.64
Proceeds of note collected by the bank which had not been recorded in the Cash account	4,000.00
Interest on note collected by the bank (no book entries made0	39.40
Debit memo for Bank charges for the month of May	23.50
Deposit in Transit (June 30, 2021)	2,144.00
Customer's check returned by the bank due to lack of funds	150.00
Outstanding checks – June 30, 2021	1,631.46
Error in recording check made by our bookkeeper – check cleared in the amount of $463.00 but entered in the bank book for $436.00	

    If we wish to reconcile the bank and book balance so that the bank balance and the book balance are reconciled to a corrected balance, the corrected balance should be
    A. $20,592.64   B. $24,019.00   C. $24,531.54   D. $26,163.00

17. The Ateb Company has issued a $500,000 bond issue on January 2, 2021 at 8% interest, payable semi-annually, sold at par, with interest payable on June 30 and December 31.   17.____
    On September 30, 2021, at the close of the fiscal year of the Ateb Company, the interest expense accrual should reflect interest payable of, approximately,
    A. $10,000   B. $20,000   C. $40,000   D. $50,000

18. Assume that a new procedure requires that a particular and unvarying sequence   18.____
    of steps be followed in order to yield the desired data. You are assigned to be in charge of subordinates working with this procedure.

Which one of the following is MOST likely to impress subordinates with the importance of following the sequence of steps exactly as given?
- A. Explain the consequences of error if the procedure is not followed.
- B. Suggest how rewarding would be the feeling of finding errors before the supervisor catches them.
- C. Indicate that independent verification of their work will be done by other staff members
- D. Advise that upward career mobility usually results from following instructions exactly

19. It is essential for an experienced accountant to know approximately how long it will take him to complete a particular assignment because
    - A. his supervisors will need to obtain this information only from someone planning to perform the assignment
    - B. he must arrange his schedule to insure proper completion of the assignment consistent with agency objectives
    - C. he must measure whether he is keeping pace with others performing similar assignments
    - D. he must determine what assignments are essential and have the greatest priority within his agency

20. There are circumstances which call for special and emergency efforts by employees. You must assign your staff to make this type of effort.
    Of the following, this special type of assignment is MOST likely to succeed if the
    - A. time schedule required to complete the assignment is precisely stated but is not adhered to
    - B. employees are individually free to determine the work schedule
    - C. assignment is clearly defined
    - D. employees are individually free to use any procedure or method available to them

KEY (CORRECT ANSWERS)

1.	A	11.	A
2.	B	12.	A
3.	B	13.	B
4.	D	14.	C
5.	A	15.	B
6.	B	16.	C
7.	C	17.	A
8.	B	18.	A
9.	A	19.	B
10.	B	20.	C

ACCOUNTING

EXAMINATION SECTION
TEST 1

DIRECTIONS: Each question or incomplete statement is followed by several suggested answers or completions. Select the one that BEST answers the question or completes the statement. PRINT THE LETTER OF THE CORRECT ANSWER IN THE SPACE AT THE RIGHT.

Questions 1-5.

DIRECTIONS: Assume that you are requested to verify certain financial data with respect to the various business entities described below. This information is required to verify that tax returns and/or other financial reports submitted to your agency are correct.

In an auditing review of the income statements of several business firms (Companies X, Y, and Z), you find the financial information given below. Based upon the account balances shown, select the correct answer for the statement information requested.

Company X - Sales $ 160,000
             Opening Inventory $ 70,000
             Purchases $ 80,000
             Purchase Returns $ 1,200
             Cost of Goods Sold $ 127,000

1. The ending inventory based upon the data above is   1.____

   A. $21,800   B. $23,000   C. $24,200   D. $33,000

Company Y - Opening Inventory $ 50,000
             Purchases $ 145,000
             Ending Inventory $ 28,500
             Gross Profit $ 56,000
             Sales and Administrative Expenses $ 64,000

2. Sales for the period based upon the data above are   2.____

   A. $110,500   B. $166,500   C. $222,500   D. $286,500

Company Z - Sales for the period $ 200,000
             Net Profit   7% of Sales
             Purchases $ 180,000
             Ending Inventory $ 70,000
             Gross Profit $ 60,000

3. Cost of Goods sold for Company Z is   3.____

   A. $110,000   B. $140,000   C. $180,000   D. $250,000

4. The opening inventory of Company Z would be   4.____

   A. $10,000   B. $20,000   C. $30,000   D. $80,000

5. The operating expenses for Company Z would be   5.____

   A. $10,000   B. $14,000   C. $20,000   D. $46,000

Questions 6-8.

DIRECTIONS: The following information is taken from the books and records of a business firm:

Sales for the calendar year 2018:	$52,000
Based upon FIFO Inventory:	
Good available for Sale	$46,900
Inventory at December 31, 2018	$12,700
Based upon LIFO Inventory:	
Goods available for Sale	$46,900
Inventory at December 31, 2018	$10,400

6. If FIFO Inventory valuation is used, the Gross Profit will be

   A. $5,100   B. $15,500   C. $17,800   D. $34,200

7. If LIFO Inventory valuation method is used, the Gross Profit will be

   A. $2,300   B. $15,500   C. $17,800   D. $36,500

8. If LIFO Inventory method is used, compared with the FIFO method, the cost of goods sold will be

   A. more by $2,300   B. less by $2,300
   C. more by $10,400   D. less by $12,700

9. Which one of the following would NOT properly be classified as an asset on the balance sheet of a business firm?

   A. Investment in stock of another firm
   B. Premium cost of a three-year fire insurance policy
   C. Cash surrender value of life insurance on life of corporate officer. Policy is owned by the company and the company is the beneficiary
   D. Amounts owing to employees for services rendered

10. Which one of the following would NOT properly be classified as a current asset?

   A. Travel advances to salespeople
   B. Postage in a postage meter
   C. Cash surrender value of life insurance policy on an officer, which policy names the corporation as the beneficiary
   D. Installment notes receivable due over 18 months in accordance with normal trade practice

11. Able, Baker and Carr formed a partnership. Able contributed $10,000, Baker contributed $5,000, and Carr contributed an automobile with a fair market value of $5,000. They have no partnership agreement. The first year the partnership earned $18,000.
The partners will share the profits as follows:

   A. Able, $9,000; Baker, $4,500; Carr, $4,500
   B. Able, $6,000; Baker, $6,000; Carr, $6,000
   C. Able, $12,000; Baker, $6,000; Carr, No share
   D. Able, $8,000; Baker, $5,000; Carr, $5,000

Questions 12-13.

DIRECTIONS: Answer Questions 12 through 13 based on the information below.

The XYZ partnership had the following balance sheet as of December 31, 2018.

Cash	$ 5,000	Liabilities	$12,000
Other assets	40,000	X Capital	20,000
Total	$45,000	Y Capital	10,000
		Z Capital	3,000
		Total	$45,000

The partners shared profits equally. They decided to liquidate the partnership at December 31, 2018.

12. If the other assets were sold for $52,000, each partner will be entitled to a final cash distribution of

    A. X, $15,000; Y, $15,000; Z, $15,000
    B. X, $24,000; Y, $14,000; Z, $ 7,000
    C. X, $20,000; Y, $10,000; Z, $ 3,000
    D. X, $23,000; Y, $13,000; Z, $ 6,000

12.____

13. If the other assets were sold for $31,000, each partner will be entitled to a final cash distribution of

    A. X, $14,000; Y, $ 5,000; Z, $5,000
    B. X, $ 8,000; Y, R 8,000; Z, $8,000
    C. X, $15,000; Y, $15,000; Z, $15,000
    D. X, $17,000; Y, $ 7,000; Z, No cash share

13.____

14. Items selling for $40 for which there were 10% selling costs were purchased for inventory at $20 each. Selling prices and costs remained steady but at the date of the financial statement the market price had dropped to $16. The inventory remaining from the original purchase was written down to $16.
Of the following, it is correct to state that the

    A. cost of sales of the subsequent year will be overstated
    B. current year's income is overstated
    C. income of the following year will be overstated
    D. closing inventory of the current year is overstated

14.____

15. Dividends in arrears on a cumulative preferred stock should be reported on the balance sheet as

    A. an accrued liability
    B. restricted retained earnings
    C. an explanatory note
    D. a deduction from preferred stock

15.____

16. The effect of recording the payment of a 10% dividend paid in stock would be to

    A. *increase* the current ratio
    B. *decrease* the amount of working capital
    C. *increase* the total stockholder equity
    D. *decrease* the book value per share of stock outstanding

16.____

17. The owner of a truck which originally had cost $12,000 but now has a book value of $1,500 was offered $3,000 for it by a used truck dealer. However, the owner traded it in for a new truck listed at $19,000 and received a trade-in allowance of $4,000.
The cost basis for the new truck, following the Federal income tax rules, *properly* amounts to

   A. $15,000   B. $16,000   C. $16,500   D. $17,500

17.___

18. In planning for purchases to be made during the next month, the following information is to be used:
   - Budgeted sales for the month   73,000 units
   - Inventory at beginning of the month   19,000 units
   - Planned inventory at end of the month 14,000 units

   From the above information, the number of units to be purchased is

   A. 40,000   B. 59,000   C. 68,000   D. 78,000

18.___

19. A branch office of a company has the following plan:
   - Cash balance at beginning of the month $ 10,000
   - Planned cash balance at end of the month $ 15,000
   - Expected receipts for the month $ 180,000
   - Expected disbursements for the month $ 205,000

   In order to comply with this plan, the accountant should recommend that the branch obtain an additional allocation of

   A. $20,000   B. $25,000   C. $30,000   D. $50,000

19.___

20. A company uses the reserve method of bad debt expense and sets up a Bad Debt account at 2% of sales. The sales were $500,000. The company wrote off $7,500 in accounts receivable.
The effect of these entries on net income for the period is a(n)

   A. $2,500 increase   B. $7,500 decrease
   C. $8,000 decrease   D. $10,000 decrease

20.___

KEY (CORRECT ANSWERS)

1. A		11. B	
2. C		12. B	
3. B		13. D	
4. C		14. C	
5. D		15. C	
6. C		16. D	
7. B		17. C	
8. A		18. C	
9. D		19. C	
10. C		20. D	

TEST 2

DIRECTIONS: Each question or incomplete statement is followed by several suggested answers or completions. Select the one that BEST answers the question or completes the statement. PRINT THE LETTER OF THE CORRECT ANSWER IN THE SPACE AT THE RIGHT.

1. The Delox Corporation has applied to their bank for a $50,000 loan which they will need for 90 days. The bank grants the loan, which will be discounted at 7% interest. The Delox Corporation will receive credit in their account at the bank for (based on a 360-day year):

   A. $46,500   B. $49,125   C. $50,000   D. $50,875

1.____

Questions 2-5.

DIRECTIONS: Answer Questions 2 through 5 based on the information below.

Assume that you are reviewing some accounts of a company and find the following: The Machinery Account and the Accumulated Depreciation - Machinery Account.

MACHINERY

Jan. 1, 2015	Machine #1	20,000	July 1, 2016	6,000
Jan. 1, 2016	Machine #2	16,000		
July 1, 2016	Machine #3	12,000		
Jan. 1, 2018	Machine #4	20,000		

ACCUMULATED DEPRECIATION - MACHINERY

Dec. 31, 2015	5,000
Dec. 31, 2016	10,500

Machines are depreciated based upon a four-year life and using the straight-line method. Assume no salvage values.

On July 1, 2016, Machine #1, purchased on January 1, 2015, was sold for $6,000 cash. The bookkeeper debited Cash and credited Machinery for $6,000.

On January 1, 2018, Machine #2 was traded in for a newer model. The new Machine had a list price of $34,000. A trade-in value of $10,000 was granted. $20,000 was paid in cash and the bookkeeper debited Machinery and credited Cash for $20,000. Income-tax rules should have been applied making this entry.

If any errors were made in recording the machine values or depreciation, you are asked to correct them and determine the corrected asset values and proper accumulated depreciation.

2. As of December 31, 2015, you determine that these two accounts

   A. are correct
   B. are incorrect
   C. overstate asset book values
   D. understate asset book values

2.____

3. As of December 31, 2016, you determine that, to correct the Machinery Account Balance, you should leave it

   A. unchanged
   C. decreased by $14,000
   B. increased by $6,000
   D. decreased by $5,500

3.____

4. As of December 31, 2016, you determine that, to reflect the proper balance, the Accumulated Depreciation - Machinery account should

   A. remain unchanged
   B. be increased by $10,000
   C. be decreased by $10,000
   D. be decreased by $ 5,500

5. After the January 1, 2018 entry, you determine that the Machinery Account should, *properly*,

   A. remain unchanged
   B. reflect a corrected balance of $52,000
   C. reflect a corrected balance of $40,000
   D. reflect a corrected balance of $56,000

Questions 6-9.

DIRECTIONS: Answer Questions 6 through 9 based on the information below.

Assume that you are assigned to prepare an Audit Report Summary on the L Company. The L Company uses the accrual method and has an accounting year ending December 31. The bookkeeper of the company has made the following errors:
1. A $1,500 collection from a customer was received on December 29, 2017, but not recorded until the date of its deposit in the bank, January 4, 2018
2. A supplier's $1,900 invoice for inventory items received December 2017 was not recorded until January 2018 (Inventories at December 31, 2017 and 2018 were stated correctly, based on physical count)
3. Depreciation for 2017 was understated by $700
4. In September 2017, a $350 invoice for office supplies was charged to the Utilities Expense account. Office supplies are expensed as purchased
5. December 31, 2017, sales on account of $2,500 were recorded in January 2018, although the merchandise had been shipped and was not in the inventory

Assume that no other errors have occurred and that no correcting entries have been made. Ignore all income taxes.

6. After correcting the errors reported above, the corrected Net Income for 2017 was

   A. overstated by $100
   B. understated by $800
   C. understated by $1,800
   D. neither understated nor overstated

7. Working Capital on December 31, 2017 was

   A. understated by $600
   B. understated by $2,300
   C. understated by $1,200
   D. neither understated nor overstated

8. Total Assets on December 31, 2018 were

   A. overstated by $1,100
   B. overstated by $1,800

C. understated by $850
D. neither understated nor overstated

9. The cash balance was

   A. correct as stated originally
   B. overstated by $1,500
   C. understated by $2,500
   D. understated by $1,500

Questions 10-13.

DIRECTIONS: Answer Questions 10 through 13 based on the information below.

Salary expense was listed as a total of $27,600 for the month of June 2018. Withholding taxes were determined to be $7,250 for Income taxes and $1,170 for FICA taxes withheld from employees. Payroll deductions for employee pension fund contribution amounted to $2,500.
Assume the employer's FICA tax share is equal to the employees' and that the employer's share of pension costs is double that of the employees and the employer also pays a 3% Unemployment Insurance Tax based upon $20,000 of the wages paid. The employer pays $1,500 for health insurance plans.

10. The amount of cash that must be obtained to meet this net payroll to pay employees is

    A. $16,680   B. $19,180   C. $20,350   D. $27,600

11. The total payroll tax expense for this payroll period is

    A. $1,170   B. $1,760   C. $2,340   D. $2,940

12. The total liability for withholding and payroll taxes payable is

    A. $2,340   B. $7,250   C. $8,420   D. $10,190

13. The expense of the employer for pension and health-care fringe benefits is

    A. $1,500   B. $2,500   C. $5,000   D. $6,500

14. Currently preferred terminology for statements to be presented limits the use of the term "reserve" to

    A. an actual liability of a known amount
    B. estimated liabilities
    C. appropriations of retained earnings
    D. valuation (contra) accounts

Questions 15-16.

DIRECTIONS: Answer Questions 15 through 16 based on the following.

The Victory Corporation provides an incentive plan whereby its president receives a bonus equal to 10% of the corporate income in excess of $150,000. The bonus is based upon income before income taxes but after calculating the bonus.

15. If the income for the calendar year 2018, before income taxes and before the bonus were $480,000 and the effective tax rate is 40%, the amount of the bonus would be

A. $15,000   B. $30,000   C. $33,000   D. $48,000

16. The income tax expense for calendar year 2012 would be   16.___

A. $60,000   B. $132,000   C. $180,000   D. $192,000

Questions 17-18.

DIRECTIONS: Answer Questions 17 through 18 based on the information below.

A contract has been awarded to the low bidder. This contractor will then commence construction of a building for the total contract price of $30,000,000. The expected cost of construction is $27,510,000. You are given the additional facts:

	2016	2017	2018
Contract Price as above	$30,000,000	$30,000,000	$30,000,000
Actual Cost to date	$9,170,000	$13,755,000	$27,510,000
Estimated Cost to complete	18,340,000	13,755,000	
Estimated Total Cost	$27,510,000	$27,510,000	$27,510,000
Estimated Total Income	$2,490,000	$	$
Billings	$9,000,000	$9,000,000	$9,000,000

17. For 2016, the income to be recognized on a percentage-of-completion basis would be   17.___

A. $830,000   B. $2,490,000
C. $3,000,000   D. $9,000,000

18. For 2017, the income to be recognized by the contractor on a percentage-of-completion basis would be   18.___

A. $415,000   B. $424,500   C. $830,000   D. $1,245,000

19. If the city borrows the $9,000,000 to pay the first billing for the contract above at 10% interest for two years, and the second $9,000,000 at 7% interest for one year, then the interest costs related to this building are, approximately,   19.___

A. $630,000   B. $1,800,000
C. $2,430,000   D. $3,000,000

20. The books of the Monmouth Corporation show the following: 20.___

Average earnings for prior 3 years	2018	2017	2016
	$70,000	$75,000	$78,000
Net tangible assets	$40,000	$42,000	$50,000

If it is expected that 15% would be normal earnings on net tangible assets, then the *average* excess earnings are

A. $7,120   B. $8,333   C. $9,800   D. $10,800

21. A business showed the following figures in its accounts for the year 2018:   21.___
    Sales - $346,000
    Inventory, December 31, 2018 - $58,000
    Inventory, December 31, 2017 - $52,000
    Purchases - $274,000
    Operating Expenses - $36,000
The gross profit earned by this concern is

A. $72,000   B. $42,000   C. $66,000   D. $78,000

22. A business firm buys an article for $320, less 40% and 10%, terms 2/10 n/30, on March 18. If it pays the bill on March 27, it should pay

    A. $169.34   B. $172.80   C. $160.00   D. $156.80

23. In the partnership of Danvers and Edwards, Danvers has a capital of $10,000 and Edwards has a capital of $15,000. If Furgal wishes to invest $11,000 and thereby receive a 1/4 interest in the business, the goodwill in the business has been computed to be worth

    A. $19,000   B. $33,000   C. $14,000   D. $8,000

24. George Bailey's capital at the beginning of the year was $14,000. At the end of the year his assets were $62,000 and his liabilities were $39,000. His drawings for the year amounted to $6,000.
    His profit for the year was

    A. $15,000   B. $3,000   C. $9,000   D. $17,000

25. George Wilson's check book shows the following:

    Balance at the beginning of the month   -$3,517.42
    Deposits during the month   -$1,923.98
    Checks drawn during the month   -$2,144.36

    In going over his bank statement, he finds that a deposit of $455.64 made by him has not yet been credited by the bank and that the bank has charged him $9.40 for services rendered. He also finds that he has outstanding checks totaling $268.19.
    His bank statement balance should be printed as

    A. $3,100.19   B. $3,118.99   C. $2,563.81   D. $4,011.47

KEY (CORRECT ANSWERS)

1. B   11. B
2. A   12. D
3. C   13. D
4. C   14. C
5. C   15. B

6. A   16. C
7. A   17. A
8. B   18. A
9. D   19. C
10. A   20. B

21. D
22. A
23. D
24. A
25. A

EXAMINATION SECTION
TEST 1

DIRECTIONS: Each question or incomplete statement is followed by several suggested answers or completions. Select the one that BEST answers the question or completes the statement. *PRINT THE LETTER OF THE CORRECT ANSWER IN THE SPACE AT THE RIGHT.*

1. In a statement of support, revenue, and expenses and changes in fund balances of a voluntary health and welfare organization, depreciation expense should

    A. not be included
    B. be included as an element of support
    C. be included as an element of other changes in fund balances
    D. be included as an element of expense

1.____

2. Which of the following NORMALLY would be included in Other Operating Revenues of a hospital?

	Revenue from educational programs	Unrestricted gifts
A.	Yes	No
B.	Yes	Yes
C.	No	Yes
D.	No	No

2.____

3. In the comprehensive annual financial report (CAFR) of a governmental unit, the account groups are included in

    A. both the combined balance sheet and the combined statement of revenues, expenditures, and changes in fund balances
    B. the combined statement of revenues, expenditures, and changes in fund balances, but not the combined balance sheet
    C. the combined balance sheet but not the combined statement of revenues, expenditures, and changes in fund balances
    D. neither the combined balance sheet nor the combined statement of revenues, expenditures, and changes in fund balances

3.____

4. Funds which the governing board of an institution, rather than a donor or other outside agency, has determined are to be retained and invested for other than loan or plant purposes would be accounted for in the

    A. quasi-endowment fund   B. endowment fund
    C. agency fund   D. current fund-restricted

4.____

5. Which of the following accounts would be included in the fund equity section of the combined balance sheet of a governmental unit for the general fixed asset account group?

	Investment in general fixed assets	Fund balance reserved for encumbrances
A.	Yes	Yes
B.	Yes	No
C.	No	No
D.	No	Yes

5.____

6. Which of the following funds of a governmental unit would account for depreciation in the accounts of the fund? 6._____

   A. General
   B. Internal service
   C. Capital projects
   D. Special assessment

7. Which of the following funds of a governmental unit uses the modified accrual basis of accounting? 7._____

   A. Enterprise
   B. Internal service
   C. Capital projects
   D. Nonexpendable trust

8. The expenditures control account of a governmental unit is credited when 8._____

   A. the budgetary accounts are closed
   B. the budget is recorded
   C. supplies are purchased
   D. supplies previously encumbered are received

9. The appropriations control account of a governmental unit is credited when 9._____

   A. supplies are purchased
   B. expenditures are recorded
   C. the budget is recorded
   D. the budgetary accounts are closed

10. Under the modified accrual basis of accounting for a governmental unit, revenues should be recognized in the accounting period in which they 10._____

    A. are earned and become measurable
    B. are collected
    C. become available and earned
    D. become available and measurable

11. How would the following be used in the economic order quantity formula? 11._____

	Inventory carrying cost	Cost per purchase order
A.	Numerator	Numerator
B.	Denominator	Numerator
C.	Denominator	Denominator
D.	Not used	Denominator

12. A company's rate of return on investment is the _____ by the capital-employed turnover rate. 12._____

    A. percentage of profit to sales divided
    B. percentage of profit to sales multiplied
    C. investment capital divided
    D. investment capital multiplied

13. A proposed project has an expected economic life of eight years. In the calculation of the net present value of the proposed project, salvage value would be

    A. excluded from the calculation of the net present value
    B. included as a cash inflow at the estimated salvage value
    C. included as a cash inflow at the future amount of the estimated salvage value
    D. included as a cash inflow at the present value of the estimated salvage value

14. Breakeven analysis assumes over the relevant range that

    A. total costs are linear
    B. fixed costs are nonlinear
    C. variable costs are nonlinear
    D. selling prices are nonlinear

15. The flexible budget for a producing department may include

	Direct labor	Factory overhead
A.	No	Yes
B.	No	No
C.	Yes	No
D.	Yes	Yes

16. In an income statement prepared as an internal report using the absorption costing method, which of the following terms should appear?

	Contribution margin	Gross profit (margin)
A.	No	Yes
B.	No	No
C.	Yes	No
D.	Yes	Yes

17. For the purposes of cost accumulation, which of the following are identifiable as different individual products before the split-off point?

	Byproducts	Joint products
A.	Yes	Yes
B.	Yes	No
C.	No	No
D.	No	Yes

18. Under the two-variance method for analyzing factory overhead, the factory overhead applied to production is used in the computation of the

	Controllable (budget) variance	Volume variance
A.	Yes	No
B.	Yes	Yes
C.	No	Yes
D.	No	No

19. In a job order cost system, direct labor costs USUALLY are recorded initially as an increase in

    A. factory overhead applied
    B. factory overhead control
    C. finished goods control
    D. work in process control

20. In developing a factory overhead application rate for use in a process costing system, which of the following could be used in the denominator?

    A. Estimated direct labor hours
    B. Actual direct labor hours
    C. Estimated factory overhead
    D. Actual factory overhead

21. How are dividends per share for common stock used in the calculation of the following?

	Dividend per-share payout ratio	Earnings per share
A.	Numerator	Numerator
B.	Numerator	Not used
C.	Denominator	Not used
D.	Denominator	Denominator

22. An employer sponsoring a defined benefit pension plan should disclose the

	Amount of unrecognized prior service cost	Fair value of plan assets
A.	No	No
B.	No	Yes
C.	Yes	Yes
D.	Yes	No

23. An investment in marketable securities was accounted for by the cost method. These securities were distributed to stockholders as a property dividend in a nonreciprocal transfer.
    The dividend should be reported at the

    A. fair value of the asset transferred
    B. fair value of the asset transferred or the recorded amount of the asset transferred, whichever is higher
    C. fair value of the asset transferred or the recorded amount of the asset transferred, whichever is lower
    D. recorded amount of the asset transferred

24. A development stage enterprise

    A. issues an income statement that is the same as an established operating enterprise, and shows cumulative amounts from the enterprise's inception as additional information
    B. issues an income statement that is the same as an established operating enterprise, but does not show cumulative amounts from the enterprise's inception as additional information
    C. issues an income statement that only shows cumulative amounts from the enterprise's inception
    D. does not issue an income statement

25. An inventory loss from a market price decline occurred in the first quarter. The loss was not expected to be restored in the fiscal year. However, in the third quarter the inventory had a market price recovery that exceeded the market decline that occurred in the first quarter.
For interim financial reporting, the dollar amount of net inventory should

   A. decrease in the first quarter by the amount of the market price decline and increase in the third quarter by the amount of the market price recovery
   B. decrease in the first quarter by the amount of the market price decline and increase in the third quarter by the amount of decrease in the first quarter
   C. not be affected in the first quarter and increase in the third quarter by the amount of the market price recovery that exceeded the amount of the market price decline
   D. not be affected in either the first quarter or the third quarter

25.____

26. When Dubke retired from the partnership of Dubke, Logan and Flaherty, the final settlement of Dubke's partnership interest exceeded Dubke's capital balance.
Under the bonus method, the excess

   A. was recorded as goodwill
   B. was recorded as an expense
   C. had no effect on the capital balances of Logan and Flaherty
   D. reduced the capital balances of Logan and Flaherty

26.____

27. A company issued rights to its existing shareholders to purchase, for $30 per share, unissued shares of $15 par value common stock.
Additional paid-in capital will be credited when the

	Rights are issued	Rights lapse
A.	Yes	No
B.	No	No
C.	No	Yes
D.	Yes	Yes

27.____

28. Five thousand (5,000) shares of common stock with a par value of $10 per share were issued initially at $12 per share. Subsequently, one thousand (1,000) of these shares were acquired as treasury stock at $15 per share. Assuming that the par value method of accounting for treasury stock transactions is used, what is the effect of the acquisition of the treasury stock on each of the following?

	Additional paid-in capital	Retained earnings
A.	Increase	No effect
B.	Increase	Decrease
C.	Decrease	Increase
D.	Decrease	Decrease

28.____

29. In determining primary earnings per share, a common stock equivalent was antidilutive in 2015 and dilutive in 2016.
The common stock equivalent would be included in the computation for

	2015	2016
A.	Yes	Yes
B.	No	Yes
C.	No	No
D.	Yes	No

29.____

30. The deferred method of tax allocation should be used for

	Permanent differences	Timing differences
A.	Yes	No
B.	Yes	Yes
C.	No	Yes
D.	No	No

KEY (CORRECT ANSWERS)

1.	D		16.	A
2.	A		17.	C
3.	C		18.	C
4.	A		19.	D
5.	B		20.	A
6.	B		21.	B
7.	C		22.	C
8.	A		23.	A
9.	C		24.	A
10.	D		25.	B
11.	B		26.	D
12.	B		27.	B
13.	D		28.	D
14.	A		29.	B
15.	D		30.	C

TEST 2

DIRECTIONS: Each question or incomplete statement is followed by several suggested answers or completions. Select the one that BEST answers the question or completes the statement. *PRINT THE LETTER OF THE CORRECT ANSWER IN THE SPACE AT THE RIGHT.*

1. When a company changes the expected service life of an asset because additional information has been obtained, which of the following should be reported?

	Cumulative effect of change in accounting principle	Pro forma effects of retroactive application
A.	Yes	No
B.	Yes	Yes
C.	No	Yes
D.	No	No

    1.____

2. Which of the following should be presented in a statement of changes in financial position prepared on a cash basis?

	Stock dividend	Stock split
A.	Yes	Yes
B.	Yes	No
C.	No	No
D.	No	Yes

    2.____

3. In a statement of changes in financial position prepared on a cash basis (indirect method), an increase in inventories should be presented as a(n)

    A. outflow of cash
    B. inflow and outflow of cash
    C. addition to income from continuing operations
    D. deduction from income from continuing operations

    3.____

4. A lease is recorded as a sales-type lease by the lessor. The difference between the gross investment in the lease and the sum of the present values of the two components of the gross investment (the net receivable) should be

    A. amortized over the period of the lease as interest revenue using the interest method
    B. amortized over the period of the lease as interest revenue using the straight-line method
    C. recognized in full as interest revenue at the lease's inception
    D. recognized in full as manufacturer's or dealer's profit at the lease's inception

    4.____

5. A company uses the percentage-of-completion method to account for a four-year construction contract.
   Progress billings sent in the second year that were collected in the third year would _____ included in the calculation of the income recognized in the _____ year.

    A. not be; second, third, or fourth
    B. be; second
    C. be; third
    D. be; fourth

    5.____

6. A material loss should be presented separately as a component of income from continuing operations when it is

    A. infrequent in occurrence and unusual in nature
    B. infrequent in occurrence but not unusual in nature
    C. a cumulative effect-type change in accounting principle
    D. an extraordinary item

7. A December 15, 2015, purchase of goods was denominated in a currency other than the entity's functional currency. The transaction resulted in a payable that was fixed in terms of the amount of foreign currency and was paid on the settlement date, January 20, 2016.
The exchange rates between the functional currency and the currency in which the transaction was denominated changed at December 31, 2015, resulting in a loss that should

    A. not be reported until January 20, 2016, the settlement date
    B. be included as a separate component of stockholders' equity at December 31, 2015
    C. be included as a deferred charge at December 31, 2015
    D. be included as a component of income from continuing operations for 2015

8. Which of the following components should be included in the calculation of net pension cost recognized for a period by an employer sponsoring a defined benefit pension plan?

	Actual return on plan assets if any	Amortization of unrecognized prior service cost, if any
A.	No	Yes
B.	No	No
C.	Yes	No
D.	Yes	Yes

9. When the interest payment dates of a bond are May 1 and November 1, and the bond is issued on June 1, 2015, the amount of interest expense for the year ended December 31, 2015 would be for _____ months.

    A. two   B. six   C. seven   D. eight

10. How would retained earnings be affected by the declaration of each of the following?

	Stock dividend	Stock split
A.	Decrease	Decrease
B.	No effect	Decrease
C.	No effect	No effect
D.	Decrease	No effect

11. A company declared a cash dividend on its common stock in December 2015, payable in January 2016.
Retained earnings would

    A. increase on the date of declaration
    B. not be affected on the date of declaration
    C. not be affected on the date of payment
    D. decrease on the date of payment

12. A safety hazard exists for a manufactured product.
Occurrence of the loss is reasonably possible, and the amount of the loss can be reasonably estimated.
This loss contingency should be

	Accrued	Disclosed
A.	Yes	Yes
B.	Yes	No
C.	No	Yes
D.	No	No

13. The proceeds from a bond issued with detachable stock purchase warrants should be accounted for

   A. entirely as bonds payable
   B. entirely as stockholders' equity
   C. partially as unearned revenue and partially as bonds payable
   D. partially as stockholders' equity and partially as bonds payable

14. A five-year term bond was issued by a company on January 1, 2015 at a premium. The carrying amount of the bond at December 31, 2016 would be

   A. the same as the carrying amount at January 1, 2015
   B. higher than the carrying amount at December 31, 2015
   C. lower than the carrying amount at December 31, 2017
   D. lower than the carrying amount at December 31, 2015

15. The market price of a bond issued at a discount is the present value of its principal amount at the market (effective) rate of interest

   A. plus the present value of all future interest payments at the market (effective) rate of interest
   B. plus the present value of all future interest payments at the rate of interest stated on the bond
   C. less the present value of all future interest payments at the market (effective) rate of interest
   D. less the present value of all future interest payments at the rate of interest stated on the bond

16. At the most recent year-end, a company had a deferred income tax credit related to a noncurrent asset that exceeded a deferred income tax charge related to a current liability.
Which of the following should be reported in the company's most recent year-end balance sheet?

   A. The excess of the deferred income tax credit over the deferred income tax charge as a noncurrent liability
   B. The excess of the deferred income tax credit over the deferred income tax charge as a current liability
   C. The deferred income tax credit as a noncurrent liability
   D. The deferred income tax credit as a current liability

17. Lease Y does not contain a bargain purchase option, but the lease term is equal to 90 percent of the estimated economic life of the leased property. Lease Z does not transfer ownership of the property to the lessee by the end of the lease term, but the lease term is equal to 75 percent of the estimated economic life of the leased property.
How should the lessee classify these leases?

	Lease Y	Lease Z
A.	Capital lease	Operating lease
B.	Capital lease	Capital lease
C.	Operating lease	Capital lease
D.	Operating lease	Operating lease

18. A six-year capital lease specifies equal minimum annual lease payments. Part of this payment represents interest and part represents a reduction in the net lease liability. The portion of the minimum lease payment in the fourth year applicable to the reduction of the net lease liability should be

   A. the same as in the third year
   B. less than in the third year
   C. less than in the fifth year
   D. more than in the fifth year

19. A retail store received cash and issued gift certificates that are redeemable in merchandise. The gift certificates lapse one year after they are issued.
How would the deferred revenue account be affected by each of the following transactions?

	Redemption of certificates	Lapse of certificates
A.	No effect	Decrease
B.	Decrease	Decrease
C.	Decrease	No effect
D.	No effect	No effect

20. Which of the following is classified as an accrued liability?

	Liability for federal unemployment taxes	Liability for employer's share of FICA taxes
A.	Yes	Yes
B.	Yes	No
C.	No	No
D.	No	Yes

21. A company borrowed cash from a bank and issued to the bank a short-term noninterest-bearing note payable. The bank discounted the note at 10% and remitted the proceeds to the company.
The effective interest rate-paid by the company in this transaction would be _____ the stated discount rate of 10%

   A. equal to
   B. more than
   C. less than
   D. independent of

22. The premium on a three-year insurance policy expiring on December 31, 2017 was paid in total on January 1, 2015. The original payment was initially debited to a prepaid asset account. The appropriate journal entry has been recorded on December 31, 2015. The balance in the prepaid asset account on December 31, 2015 should be

   A. zero
   B. the same as it would have been if the original payment had been debited initially to an expense account
   C. the same as the original payment
   D. higher than if the original payment had been debited initially to an expense account

22.____

23. The market price of the common stock of an investee company increased during the year.
   How will the investor's investment account be affected by the increase in market price of that common stock under each of the following accounting methods?

	Cost method	Equity method
A.	No effect	No effect
B.	No effect	Increase
C.	Increase	No effect
D.	Increase	Increase

23.____

24. An investor purchased a bond classified as a long-term investment between interest dates at a discount.
   At the purchase date, the carrying amount of the bond is more than the

	Cash paid to seller	Face amount of bond
A.	Yes	No
B.	Yes	Yes
C.	No	Yes
D.	No	No

24.____

25. When the market value of an investment in debt securities exceeds its carrying amount, how should the asset be reported at the end of the year for each of the following?

	Short-term marketable debt securities	Long-term marketable debt securities
A.	Carrying amount	Market
B.	Carrying amount	Carrying amount
C.	Market	Carrying amount
D.	Market	Market

25.____

26. A marketable equity securities portfolio is included in an unclassified balance sheet. The amount by which the aggregate cost of the marketable equity securities portfolio exceeds its aggregate market value should

   A. be reported as a valuation allowance in the asset section of the balance sheet
   B. be reported as a valuation allowance in the liability section of the balance sheet
   C. be reported as an unrealized loss in the income statement
   D. not be reported in the financial statements

26.____

27. When the allowance method of recognizing bad debt expense is used, the allowance for doubtful accounts would decrease when a(n)

   A. specific account receivable is collected
   B. account previously written off is collected
   C. account previously written off becomes collectible
   D. specific uncollectible account is written off

27.____

28. On July 1, 2015, a company received a one-year note receivable bearing interest at the market rate. The face amount of the note receivable and the entire amount of the interest are due on June 30, 2016.
   The interest receivable account would show a balance on

   A. July 1, 2015 but not December 31, 2015
   B. December 31, 2015 but not July 1, 2015
   C. July 1, 2015 and December 31, 2015
   D. neither July 1, 2015 nor December 31, 2015

28.____

29. When purchasing power gains or losses are computed, how is each of the following classified?

29.____

	Patents	Unamortized premium on bonds payable
A.	Nonmonetary	Monetary
B.	Nonmonetary	Nonmonetary
C.	Monetary	Nonmonetary
D.	Monetary	Monetary

30. According to the FASB conceptual framework, predictive value is an ingredient of

30.____

	Relevance	Reliability
A.	Yes	No
B.	Yes	Yes
C.	No	Yes
D.	No	No

KEY (CORRECT ANSWERS)

1.	D	16.	C
2.	C	17.	B
3.	D	18.	C
4.	A	19.	B
5.	A	20.	A
6.	B	21.	B
7.	D	22.	B
8.	D	23.	A
9.	C	24.	D
10.	D	25.	B
11.	C	26.	A
12.	C	27.	D
13.	D	28.	B
14.	D	29.	A
15.	A	30.	A

PREPARING WRITTEN MATERIAL
EXAMINATION SECTION
TEST 1

DIRECTIONS: Each of the sentences in this test may be classified under one of the following four categories:
- A. *Incorrect* because of faulty grammar or sentence structure
- B. *Incorrect* because of faulty punctuation
- C. *Incorrect* because of faulty capitalization
- D. *Correct*

Examine each sentence carefully to determine under which of the above four options it is best classified. Then, in the space at the right, print the capital letter preceding the option which is the BEST of the four suggested above.

(Each incorrect sentence contains but one type of error. Consider a sentence to be correct if it contains none of the types of errors mentioned, even though there may be other correct ways of expressing the same thought.)

1. This fact, together with those brought out at the previous meeting, prove that the schedule is satisfactory to the employees.   1.____

2. Like many employees in scientific fields, the work of bookkeepers and accountants requires accuracy and neatness.   2.____

3. "What can I do for you," the secretary asked as she motioned to the visitor to take a seat.   3.____

4. Our representative, Mr. Charles will call on you next week to determine whether or not your claim has merit.   4.____

5. We expect you to return in the spring; please do not disappoint us.   5.____

6. Any supervisor, who disregards the just complaints of his subordinates, is remiss in the performance of his duty.   6.____

7. Because she took less than an hour for lunch is no reason for permitting her to leave before five o'clock.   7.____

8. "Miss Smith," said the supervisor, "Please arrange a meeting of the staff for two o'clock on Monday."   8.____

9. A private company's vacation and sick leave allowance usually differs considerably from a public agency.   9.____

10. Therefore, in order to increase the efficiency of operations in the department, a report on the recommended changes in procedures was presented to the departmental committee in charge of the program.   10.____

81

11. We told him to assign the work to whoever was available. 11._____

12. Since John was the most efficient of any other employee in the bureau, he received the highest service rating. 12._____

13. Only those members of the national organization who resided in the middle West attended the conference in Chicago. 13._____

14. The question of whether the office manager has as yet attained, or indeed can ever hope to secure professional status is one which has been discussed for years. 14._____

15. No one knew who to blame for the error which, we later discovered, resulted in a considerable loss of time. 15._____

KEY (CORRECT ANSWERS)

1.	A	6.	B	11.	D
2.	A	7.	A	12.	A
3.	B	8.	C	13.	C
4.	B	9.	A	14.	B
5.	D	10.	D	15.	A

TEST 2

DIRECTIONS: Each of the sentences in this test may be classified under one of the following four categories:
  A. *Incorrect* because of faulty grammar or sentence structure
  B. *Incorrect* because of faulty punctuation
  C. *Incorrect* because of faulty capitalization
  D. *Correct*

1. The National alliance of Businessmen is trying to persuade private businesses to hire youth in the summertime.   1.____

2. The supervisor who is on vacation, is in charge of processing vouchers.   2.____

3. The activity of the committee at its conferences is always stimulating.   3.____

4. After checking the addresses again, the letters went to the mailroom.   4.____

5. The director, as well as the employees, are interested in sharing the dividends.   5.____

KEY (CORRECT ANSWERS)

1. C
2. B
3. D
4. A
5. A

TEST 3

DIRECTIONS: In each of the following groups of sentences, one of the four sentences is faulty in grammar, punctuation, or capitalization. Select the INCORRECT sentence in each case.

1. A. Sailing down the bay was a thrilling experience for me.
   B. He was not consulted about your joining the club.
   C. This story is different than the one I told you yesterday.
   D. There is no doubt about his being the best player.

2. A. He maintains there is but one road to world peace.
   B. It is common knowledge that a child sees much he is not supposed to see.
   C. Much of the bitterness might have been avoided if arbitration had been resorted to earlier in the meeting.
   D. The man decided it would be advisable to marry a girl somewhat younger than him.

3. A. In this book, the incident I liked least is where the hero tries to put out the forest fire.
   B. Learning a foreign language will undoubtedly give a person a better understanding of his mother tongue.
   C. His actions made us wonder what he planned to do next.
   D. Because of the war, we were unable to travel during the summer vacation.

4. A. The class had no sooner become interested in the lesson than the dismissal bell rang.
   B. There is little agreement about the kind of world to be planned at the peace conference.
   C. "Today," said the teacher, "we shall read 'The Wind in the Willows,' I am sure you'll like it.
   D. The terms of the legal settlement of the family quarrel handicapped both sides for many years.

5. A. I was so surprised that I was not able to say a word.
   B. She is taller than any other member of the class.
   C. It would be much more preferable if you were never seen in his company.
   D. We had no choice but to excuse her for being late.

KEY (CORRECT ANSWERS)

1. C
2. D
3. A
4. C
5. C

TEST 4

DIRECTIONS: In each of the following groups of sentences, one of the four sentences is faulty in grammar, punctuation, or capitalization. Select the INCORRECT sentence in each case.

1. A. Please send me these data at the earliest opportunity.
   B. The loss of their material proved to be a severe handicap.
   C. My principal objection to this plan is that it is impracticable.
   D. The doll had laid in the rain for an hour and was ruined.

   1.____

2. A. The garden scissors, left out all night in the rain, were in a badly rusted condition.
   B. The girls felt bad about the misunderstanding which had arisen
   C. Sitting near the campfire, the old man told John and I about many exciting adventures he had had.
   D. Neither of us is in a position to undertake a task of that magnitude.

   2.____

3. A. The general concluded that one of the three roads would lead to the besieged city.
   B. The children didn't, as a rule, do hardly anything beyond what they were told to do.
   C. The reason the girl gave for her negligence was that she had acted on the spur of the moment.
   D. The daffodils and tulips look beautiful in that blue vase.

   3.____

4. A. If I was ten years older, I should be interested in this work.
   B. Give the prize to whoever has drawn the best picture.
   C. When you have finished reading the book, take it back to the library.
   D. My drawing is as good as or better than yours.

   4.____

5. A. He asked me whether the substance was animal or vegetable.
   B. An apple which is unripe should not be eaten by a child.
   C. That was an insult to me who am your friend.
   D. Some spy must of reported the matter to the enemy.

   5.____

6. A. Limited time makes quoting the entire message impossible.
   B. Who did she say was going?
   C. The girls in your class have dressed more dolls this year than we.
   D. There was such a large amount of books on the floor that I couldn't find a place for my rocking chair.

   6.____

7. A. What with his sleeplessness and his ill health, he was unable to assume any responsibility for the success of the meeting.
   B. If I had been born in February, I should be celebrating my birthday soon.
   C. In order to prevent breakage, she placed a sheet of paper between each of the plates when she packed them.
   D. After the spring shower, the violets smelled very sweet.

   7.____

8. A. He had laid the book down very reluctantly before the end of the lesson.
    B. The dog, I am sorry to say, had lain on the bed all night.
    C. The cloth was first lain on a flat surface; then it was pressed with a hot iron.
    D. While we were in Florida, we lay in the sun until we were noticeably tanned.

    8.____

9. A. If John was in New York during the recent holiday season, I have no doubt he spent most of the time with his parents.
    B. How could he enjoy the television program; the dog was barking and the baby was crying.
    C. When the problem was explained to the class, he must have been asleep.
    D. She wished that her new dress were finished so that she could go to the party.

    9.____

10. A. The engine not only furnishes power but light and heat as well.
    B. You're aware that we've forgotten whose guilt was established, aren't you?
    C. Everybody knows that the woman made many sacrifices for her children.
    D. A man with his dog and gun is a familiar sight in this neighborhood.

    10.____

KEY (CORRECT ANSWERS)

1. D 6. D
2. C 7. B
3. B 8. C
4. A 9. B
5. D 10. A

TEST 5

DIRECTIONS: Each of Questions 1 through 5 consists of a sentence which may be classified appropriately under one of the following four categories:
    A. *Incorrect* because of faulty grammar
    B. *Incorrect* because of faulty punctuation
    C. *Incorrect* because of faulty spelling
    D. *Correct*

Examine each sentence carefully. Then, print in the space at the right the letter preceding the category which is the BEST of the four suggested above
(Note: Each incorrect sentence contains only one type of error. Consider a sentence correct if it contains no errors, although there may be other correct ways of writing the sentence.)

1. Of the two employees, the one in our office is the most efficient.   1.____

2. No one can apply or even understand, the new rules and regulations.   2.____

3. A large amount of supplies were stored in the empty office.   3.____

4. If an employee is occassionally asked to work overtime, he should do so willingly.   4.____

5. It is true that the new procedures are difficult to use but, we are certain that you will learn them quickly.   5.____

6. The office manager said that he did not know who would be given a large allotment under the new plan.   6.____

7. It was at the supervisor's request that the clerk agreed to postpone his vacation.   7.____

8. We do not believe that it is necessary for both he and the clerk to attend the conference.   8.____

9. All employees, who display perseverance, will be given adequate recognition.   9.____

10. He regrets that some of us employees are dissatisfied with our new assignments.   10.____

11. "Do you think that the raise was merited," asked the supervisor?   11.____

12. The new manual of procedure is a valuable supplament to our rules and regulations.   12.____

13. The typist admitted that she had attempted to pursuade the other employees to assist her in her work.   13.____

2 (#5)

14. The supervisor asked that all amendments to the regulations be handled by you and I.   14.____

15. The custodian seen the boy who broke the window.   15.____

KEY (CORRECT ANSWERS)

1.	A	6.	D	11.	B
2.	B	7.	D	12.	C
3.	A	8.	A	13.	C
4.	C	9.	B	14.	A
5.	B	10.	D	15.	A

PREPARING WRITTEN MATERIAL

PARAGRAPH REARRANGEMENT
COMMENTARY

The sentences that follow are in scrambled order. You are to rearrange them in proper order and indicate the letter choice containing the correct answer at the space at the right.

Each group of sentences in this section is actually a paragraph presented in scrambled order. Each sentence in the group has a place in that paragraph; no sentence is to be left out. You are to read each group of sentences and decide upon the best order in which to put the sentences so as to form a well-organized paragraph.

The questions in this section measure the ability to solve a problem when all the facts relevant to its solution are not given.

More specifically, certain positions of responsibility and authority require the employee to discover connection between events sometimes, apparently, unrelated. In order to do this, the employee will find it necessary to correctly infer that unspecified events have probably occurred or are likely to occur. This ability becomes especially important when action must be taken on incomplete information.

Accordingly, these questions require competitors to choose among several suggested alternatives, each of which presents a different sequential arrangement of the events. Competitors must choose the MOST logical of the suggested sequences.

In order to do so, they may be required to draw on general knowledge to infer missing concepts or events that are essential to sequencing the given events. Competitors should be careful to infer only what is essential to the sequence. The plausibility of the wrong alternatives will always require the inclusion of unlikely events or of additional chains of events which are NOT essential to sequencing the given events.

It's very important to remember that you are looking for the best of the four possible choices, and that the best choice of all may not even be one of the answers you're given to choose from.

There is no one right way to solve these problems. Many people have found it helpful to first write out the order of the sentences, as they would have arranged them, on their scrap paper before looking at the possible answers. If their optimum answer is there, this can save them some time. If it isn't, this method can still give insight into solving the problem. Others find it most helpful to just go through each of the possible choices, contrasting each as they go along. You should use whatever method feels comfortable and works for you.

While most of these types of questions are not that difficult, we've added a higher percentage of the difficult type, just to give you more practice. Usually there are only one or two questions on this section that contain such subtle distinctions that you're unable to answer confidently. And you then may find yourself stuck deciding between two possible choices, neither of which you're sure about.

EXAMINATION SECTION
TEST 1

DIRECTIONS: The following groups of sentences need to be arranged in an order that makes sense. Select the letter preceding the sequence that represents the BEST sentence order. *PRINT THE LETTER OF THE CORRECT ANSWER IN THE SPACE AT THE RIGHT.*

1. I. The keyboard was purposely designed to be a little awkward to slow typists down.
    II. The arrangement of letters on the keyboard of a typewriter was not designed for the convenience of the typist.
    III. Fortunately, no one is suggesting that a new keyboard be designed right away.
    IV. If one were, we would have to learn to type all over again.
    V. The reason was that the early machines were slower than the typists and would jam easily.
    The CORRECT answer is:
    A. I, III, IV, II, V
    B. II, V, I, IV, III
    C. V, I, II, III, IV
    D. II, I, V, III, IV

    1.____

2. I. The majority of the new service jobs are part-time or low-paying.
    II. According to the U.S. Bureau of Labor Statistics, jobs in the service sector constitute 72% of all jobs in this country.
    III. If more and more workers receive less and less money, who will buy the goods and services needed to keep the economy going?
    IV. The service sector is by far the fastest growing part of the United States economy.
    V. Some economists look upon this trend with great concern.
    The CORRECT answer is:
    A. II, IV, I, V, III
    B. II, III, IV, I, V
    C. V, IV, II, III, I
    D. III, I, II, IV, V

    2.____

3. I. They can also affect one's endurance.
    II. This can stabilize blood sugar levels, and ensure that the brain is receiving a steady, constant, supply of glucose, so that one is *hitting on all cylinders* while taking the test.
    III. By food, we mean real food, not junk food or unhealthy snacks.
    IV. For this reason, it is important not to skip a meal, and to bring food with you to the exam.
    V. One's blood sugar levels can affect how clearly one is able to think and concentrate during an exam.
    The CORRECT answer is:
    A. V, II, III, I
    B. V, II, I, IV, III
    C. V, I, IV, III, II
    D. V, IV, I, III, II

    3.____

4.
I. Those who are the embodiment of desire are absorbed in material quests, and those who are the embodiment of feeling are warriors who value power more than possession.
II. These qualities are in everyone, but in different degrees.
III. But those who value understanding yearn not for goods or victory, but for knowledge.
IV. According to Plato, human behavior flows from three main sources: desire, emotion, and knowledge.
V. In the perfect state, the industrial forces would produce but not rule, the military would protect but not rule, and the forces of knowledge, the philosopher kings, would reign.

The CORRECT answer is:
A. IV, V, I, II, III
B. V, I, II, III, IV
C. IV, III, II, I, V
D. IV, II, I, III, V

5.
I. Of the more than 26,000 tons of garbage produced daily in New York City, 12,000 tons arrive daily at Fresh Kills.
II. In a month, enough garbage accumulates there to fill the Empire State Building.
III. In 1937, the Supreme Court halted the practice of dumping the trash of New York City into the sea.
IV. Although the garbage is compacted, in a few years the mounds of garbage at Fresh Kills will be the highest points south of Maine's Mount Desert Island on the Eastern Seaboard.
V. Instead, tugboats now pull barges of much of the trash to Staten Island and the largest landfill in the world, Fresh Kills.

The CORRECT answer is:
A. III, V, IV, I, II
B. III, V, II, IV, I
C. III, V, I, II, IV
D. III, II, V, IV, I

6.
I. Communists rank equality very high, but freedom very low.
II. Unlike communists, conservatives place a high value on freedom and a very low value on equality.
III. A recent study demonstrated that one way to classify people's political beliefs is to look at the importance placed on two words: freedom and equality.
IV. Thus, by demonstrating how members of these groups feel about the two words, the study has proved to be useful for political analysts in several European countries.
V. According to the study, socialists and liberals rank both freedom and equality very high, while fascists rate both very low.

The CORRECT answer is:
A. III, V, I, II, IV
B. V, IV, III, I, II
C. III, V, IV, II, I
D. III, I, II, IV, V

7. I. "Can there be anything more amazing than this?"
    II. If the riddle is successfully answered, his dead brothers will be brought back to life.
    III. "Even though man sees those around him dying every day," says Dharmaraj, "he still believes and acts as if he were immortal."
    IV. "What is the cause of ceaseless wonder?" asks the Lord of the Lake.
    V. In the ancient epic, The Mahabharata, a riddle is asked of one of the Pandava brothers.
    The CORRECT answer is:
    A. V, II, I, IV, III
    B. V, IV, III, I, II
    C. V, II, IV, III, I
    D. V, II, IV, I, III

7.____

8. I. On the contrary, the two main theories—the cooperative (neoclassical) theory and the radical (labor theory)—clearly rest on very different assumptions, which have very different ethical overtones.
    II. The distribution of income is the primary factor in determining the relative levels of material well-being that different groups or individuals attain.
    III. Of all issues in economics, the distribution of income is one of the most controversial.
    IV. The neoclassical theory tends to support the existing income distribution (or minor changes), while the labor theory ends to support substantial changes in the way income is distributed.
    V. The intensity of the controversy reflects the fact that different economic theories are not purely neutral, *detached* theories with no ethical or moral implications.
    The CORRECT answer is:
    A. II, I, V, IV, III
    B. III, II, V, I, IV
    C. III, V, II, I, IV
    D. III, V, IV, I, II

8.____

9. I. The pool acts as a broker and ensures that the cheapest power gets used first.
    II. Every six seconds, the pool's computer monitors all of the generating stations in the state and decides which to ask for more power and which to cut back.
    III. The buying and selling of electrical power is handled by the New York Power Pool in Guilderland, New York.
    IV. This is to the advantage of both the buying and selling utilities.
    V. The pool began operation in 1970, and consists of the state's eight electric utilities.
    The CORRECT answer is:
    A. V, I, II, III, IV
    B. IV, II, I, III, V
    C. III, V, I, IV, II
    D. V, III, IV, II, I

9.____

10. I. Modern English is much simpler grammatically than Old English. 10.____
    II. Finnish grammar is very complicated; there are some fifteen cases, for example.
    III. Chinese, a very old language, may seem to be the exception, but it is the great number of characters/words that must be mastered that makes it so difficult to learn, not its grammar.
    IV. The newest literary language—that is, written as well as spoken—is Finish, whose literary roots go back only to about the middle of the nineteenth century.
    V. Contrary to popular belief, the longer a language is been in use the simpler its grammar—not the reverse.
    The CORRECT answer is:
    A. IV, I, II, III, V
    B. V, I, IV, II, III
    C. I, II, IV, III, V
    D. IV, II, III, I, V

KEY (CORRECT ANSWERS)

1.	D	6.	A
2.	A	7.	C
3.	C	8.	B
4.	D	9.	C
5.	C	10.	B

TEST 2

DIRECTIONS: This type of question tests your ability to recognize accurate paraphrasing, well-constructed paragraphs, and appropriate style and tone. It is important that the answer you select contains only the facts or concepts given in the original sentences. It is also important that you be aware of incomplete sentences, inappropriate transitions, unsupported opinions, incorrect usage, and illogical sentence order. Paragraphs that do not include all the necessary facts and concepts, that distort them, or that add new ones are not considered correct.

The format for this section may vary. Sometimes, long paragraphs are given, and emphasis is placed on style and organization. Our first five questions are of this type. Other times, the paragraphs are shorter, and there is less emphasis on style and more emphasis on accurate representation of information. Our second group of five questions are of this nature.

For each of Questions 1 through 10, select the paragraph that BEST expresses the ideas contained in the sentences above it. *PRINT THE LETTER OF THE CORRECT ANSWER IN THE SPACE AT THE RIGHT.*

1. I. Listening skills are very important for managers.
    II. Listening skills are not usually emphasized.
    III. Whenever managers are depicted in books, manuals or the media, they are always talking, never listening.
    IV. We'd like you to read the enclosed handout on listening skills and to try to consciously apply them this week.
    V. We guarantee they will improve the quality of your interactions.

    A. Unfortunately, listening skills are not usually emphasized for managers. Managers are always depicted as talking, never listening. We'd like you to read the enclosed handout on listening skills. Please try to apply these principles this week. If you do, we guarantee they will improve the quality of your interactions.
    B. The enclosed handout on listening skills will be important improving the quality of your interactions. We guarantee it. All you have to do is take sometime this week to read and to consciously try to apply the principles. Listening skills are very important for manages, but they are not usually emphasized. Whenever managers are depicted in books, manuals or the media, they are always talking, never listening.
    C. Listening well is one of the most important skills a manager can have, yet it's not usually given much attention. Think about any representation of managers in books, manuals, or in the media that you may have seen. They're always talking, never listening. We'd like you to read the enclosed handout on listening skills and consciously try to apply them the rest of the week. We guarantee you will see a difference in the quality of your interactions.

1.____

D. Effective listening, one very important tool in the effective manager's arsenal, is usually not emphasized enough. The usual depiction of managers in books, manuals or the media is one in which they are always talking, never listening. We'd like you to read the enclosed handout and consciously try to apply the information contained therein throughout the rest of the week. We feel sure that you will see a marked difference in the quality of your interactions.

2. I. Chekhov wrote three dramatic masterpieces which share certain themes and formats: <u>Uncle Vanya</u>, <u>The Cherry Orchard</u>, and <u>The Three Sisters</u>.
   II. They are primarily concerned with the passage of time and how this erodes human aspirations.
   III. The plays are haunted by the ghosts of the wasted life.
   IV. The characters are concerned with life's lesser problems; however, such as the inability to make decisions, loyalty to the wrong cause, and the inability to be clear.
   V. This results in sweet, almost aching, type of a sadness referred to as Chekhovian.

2.____

   A. Chekhov wrote three dramatic masterpieces: <u>Uncle Vanya</u>, <u>The Cherry Orchard</u>, and <u>The Three Sisters</u>. These masterpieces share certain themes and formats: the passage of time, how time erodes human aspirations, and the ghosts of wasted life. Each masterpiece is characterized by a sweet, almost aching, type of sadness that has become known as Chekhovian. The sweetness of this sadness hinges on the fact that it is not the great tragedies of life which are destroying these characters, but their minor flaws: indecisiveness, misplaced loyalty, unclarity.
   B. <u>The Cherry Orchard</u>, <u>Uncle Vanya</u>, and <u>The Three Sisters</u> are three dramatic masterpieces written by Chekhov that use similar formats to explore a common theme. Each is primarily concerned with the way that passing time wears down human aspirations, and each is haunted by the ghosts of the wasted life. The characters are shown struggling futilely with the lesser problems of life: indecisiveness, loyalty to the wrong cause, and the inability to be clear. These struggles create a mood of sweet, almost aching, sadness that has become known as Chekhovian.
   C. Chekhov's dramatic masterpieces are, along with <u>The Cherry Orchard</u>, <u>Uncle Vanya</u>, and <u>The Three Sisters</u>. These plays share certain thematic and formal similarities. They are concerned most of all with the passage of time and the way in which time erodes human aspirations. Each play is haunted by the specter of the wasted life. Chekhov's characters are caught, however, by life's lesser snares: indecisiveness, loyalty to the wrong cause, and unclarity. The characteristic mood is a sweet, almost aching type of sadness that has come to be known as Chekhovian.
   D. A Chekhovian mood is characterized by sweet, almost aching, sadness. The term comes from three dramatic tragedies by Chekhov which revolve around the sadness of a wasted life. The three masterpieces (<u>Uncle Vanya</u>, <u>The Three Sisters</u>, and <u>The Cherry Orchard</u>) share the same

theme and format. The plays are concerned with how the passage of time erodes human aspirations. They are peopled with characters who are struggling with life's lesser problems. These are people who are indecisive, loyal to the wrong causes, or are unable to make themselves clear.

3.
- I. Movie previews have often helped producers decide which parts of movies they should take out or leave in.
- II. The first 1933 preview of King Kong was very helpful to the producers because many people ran screaming from the theater and would not return when four men first attacked by Kong were eaten by giant spiders.
- III. The 1950 premiere of Sunset Boulevard resulted in the filming of an entirely new beginning, and a delay of six months in the film's release.
- IV. In the original opening scene, William Holden was in a morgue talking with thirty-six other "corpses" about the ways some of them had died.
- V. When he began to tell them of his life with Gloria Swanson, the audience found this hilarious, instead of taking the scene seriously.

3.____

   A. Movie previews have often helped producers decide what parts of movies they should leave in or take out. For example, the first preview of King Kong in 1933 was very helpful. In one scene, four men were first attacked by Kong and then eaten by giant spiders. Many members of the audience ran screaming from the theater and would not return. The premiere of the 1950 film Sunset Boulevard was also very helpful. In the original opening scene, William Holden was in a morgue with thirty-six other "corpses," discussing the ways some of them had died. When he began to tell them of his life with Gloria Swanson, the audience found this hilarious. They were supposed to take the scene seriously. The result was a delay of six months in the release of the film while a new beginning was added.
   B. Movie previews have often helped producers decide whether they should change various parts of a movie. After the 1933 preview of King Kong, a scene in which four men who had been attacked by Kong were eaten by giant spiders was taken out as many people ran screaming from the theater and would not return. The 1950 premiere of Sunset Boulevard also led to some changes. In the original opening scene, William Holden was in a morgue talking with thirty-six other "corpses" about the ways some of them had died. When he began to tell them of his life with Gloria Swanson, the audience found this hilarious, instead of taking the scene seriously.
   C. What do Sunset Boulevard and King Kong have in common? Both show the value of using movie previews to test audience reaction. The first 1933 preview of King Kong showed that a scene showing four men being eaten by giant spiders after having been attacked by Kong was too frightening for many people. They ran screaming from the theater and couldn't be coaxed back. The 1950 premiere of Sunset Boulevard was also a scream, but not the kind the producers intended. The movie opens

with William Holden lying in a morgue discussing the ways they had died with thirty-six other "corpses." When he began to tell them of his life with Gloria Swanson, the audience couldn't take him seriously. Their laughter caused a six-month delay while the beginning was rewritten.

D. Producers very often use movie previews to decide if changes are needed. The premiere of Sunset Boulevard in 1950 led to a new beginning and a six-month delay in film release. At the beginning, William Holden and thirty-six other "corpses" discuss the ways some of them died. Rather than taking this seriously, the audience thought it was hilarious when he began to tell them of his life with Gloria Swanson. The first 1933 preview of King Kong was very helpful for its producers because one scene so terrified the audience that many of them ran screaming from the theater and would not return. In this particular scene, four men who had first been attacked by Kong were eaten by giant spiders.

4.
I. It is common for supervisors to view employees as "things" to be manipulated.
II. This approach does not motivate employees, nor does the carrot-and-stick approach because employees often recognize these behaviors and resent them.
III. Supervisors can change these behaviors by using self-inquiry and persistence.
IV. The best managers genuinely respect those they work with, are supportive and helpful, and are interested in working as a team with those they supervise.
V. They disagree with the Golden Rule that says "he or she who has the gold makes the rules."

4.____

A. Some managers act as if they think the Golden Rule means "he or she who has the gold makes the rules." They show disrespect to employees by seeing them as "things" to be manipulated. Obviously, this approach does not motivate employees any more than the carrot-and-stick approach motivates them. The employees are smart enough to spot these behaviors and resent them. On the other hand, the managers genuinely respect those they work with, are supportive and helpful, and are interested in working as a team. Self-inquiry and persistence can change even the former type of supervisor into the latter.

B. Many supervisors all into the trap of viewing employees as "things" to be manipulated, or try to motivate them by using a carrot-and-stick approach. These methods do not motivate employees, who often recognize the behaviors and resent them. Supervisors can change these behaviors, however, by using self-inquiry and persistence. The best managers are supportive and helpful, and have genuine respect for those with whom they work. They are interested in working as a team with those they supervise. To them, the Golden Rule is not "he or she who has the gold makes the rules."

C. Some supervisors see employees as "things" to be used or manipulated using a carrot-and-stick technique. These methods don't work. Employees often see through them and resent them. A supervisor who wants to change may do so. The techniques of self-inquiry and persistence can be used to turn him or her into the type of supervisor who doesn't think the Golden Rule is "he or she who has the gold makes the rules." They may become like the best managers who treat those with whom they work with respect and give them help and support. These are the manager who know how to build a team.

D. Unfortunately, many supervisors act as if their employees are objects whose movements they can position at will. This mistaken belief has the same result as another popular motivational technique—the carrot-and-stick approach. Both attitudes can lead to the same result—resentment from those employees who recognize the behaviors for what they are. Supervisors who recognize these behaviors can change through the use of persistence and the use of self-inquiry. It's important to remember that the best managers respect their employees. They readily give necessary help and support and are interested in working as a team with those they supervise. To these managers, the Golden Rule is not "he or she who has the gold makes the rules."

5. I. The first half of the nineteenth century produced a group of pessimistic poets—Byron, De Musset, Heine, Pushkin, and Leopardi.
    II. It also produced a group of pessimistic composers—Schubert, Chopin, Schumann, and even the later Beethoven.
    III. Above all, in philosophy, there was the profoundly pessimistic philosopher, Schopenhauer.
    IV. The Revolution was dead, the Bourbons were restored, the feudal barons were reclaiming their land, and progress everywhere was being suppressed, as the great age was over.
    V. "I thank God," said Goethe, "that I am not young in so thoroughly finished a world."

    A. "I thank God," said Goethe, "that I am not young in so thoroughly finished a world." The Revolution was dead, the Bourbons were restored, the feudal barons were reclaiming their land, and progress everywhere was being suppressed. The first half of the nineteenth century produced a group of pessimistic poets: Byron, De Musset, Heine, Pushkin, and Leopardi. It also produced pessimistic composers: Schubert, Chopin, Schumann. Although Beethoven came later, he fits into this group, too. Finally and above all, it also produced a profoundly pessimistic philosopher, Schopenhauer. The great age was over.
    B. The first half of the nineteenth century produced a group of pessimistic poets: Byron, De Musset, Heine, Pushkin, and Leopardi. It produced a group of pessimistic composers: Schubert, Chopin, Schumann, and even the later Beethoven. Above all, it produced a profoundly pessimistic philosopher, Schopenhauer. For each of these men, the great age was over. The Revolution was dead, and the Bourbons were restored. The feudal barons were reclaiming their land, and progress everywhere was being suppressed.

5._____

C. The great age was over. The Revolution was dead—the Bourbons were restored, and the feudal barons were reclaiming their land. Progress everywhere was being suppressed. Out of this climate came a profound pessimism. Poets, like Byron, De Musset, Heine, Pushkin, and Leopardi; composers, like Schubert, Chopin, Schumann, and even the later Beethoven; and above all, a profoundly pessimistic philosopher, Schopenauer. This pessimism which arose in the first half of the nineteenth century is illustrated by these words of Goethe, "I thank God that I am not young in so thoroughly finished a world."

D. The first half of the nineteenth century produced a group of pessimistic poets, Byron, De Musset, Heine, Pushkin, and Leopardi—and a group of pessimistic composers, Schubert, Chopin, Schumann, and the later Beethoven. Above it all, it produced a profoundly pessimistic philosopher, Schopenhauer. The great age was over. The Revolution was dead, the Bourbons were restored, the feudal barons were reclaiming their land, and progress everywhere was being suppressed. "I thank God," said Goethe, "that I am not young in so thoroughly finished a world."

6. I. A new manager sometimes may feel insecure about his or her competence in the new position.
   II. The new manager may then exhibit defensive or arrogant behavior towards those one supervises, or the new manager may direct overly flattering behavior toward one's new supervisor.

6._____

   A. Sometimes, a new manager may feel insecure about his or her ability to perform well in this new position. The insecurity may lead him or her to treat others differently. He or she may display arrogant or defensive behavior towards those he or she supervises, or be overly flattering to his or her new supervisor.
   B. A new manager may sometimes feel insecure about his or her ability to perform well in the new position. He or she may then become arrogant, defensive, or overly flattering towards those he or she works with.
   C. There are times when a new manager may be insecure about how well he or she can perform in the new job. The new manager may also behave defensive or act in an arrogant way towards those he or she supervises, or overly flatter his or her boss.
   D. Sometimes a new manager may feel insecure about his or her ability to perform well in the new position. He or she may then display arrogant or defensive behavior towards those they supervise, or become overly flattering towards their supervisors.

7. I. It is possible to eliminate unwanted behavior by bringing it under stimulus control—tying the behavior to a cue, and then never, or rarely, giving the cue.
   II. One trainer successfully used this method to keep an energetic young porpoise from coming out of her tank whenever she felt like it, which was potentially dangerous.
   III. Her trainer taught her to do it for a reward, in response to a hand signal, and then rarely gave the signal.

7._____

A. Unwanted behavior can be eliminated by tying the behavior to a cue, and then never, or rarely, giving the cue. This is called stimulus control. One trainer was able to use this method to keep an energetic young porpoise from coming out of her tank by teaching her to come out for a reward in response to a hand signal, and then rarely giving the signal.
B. Stimulus control can be used to eliminate unwanted behavior. In this method, behavior is tied to a cue, and then the cue is rarely, if ever, given. One trainer was able to successfully use stimulus control to keep an energetic young porpoise from coming out of her tank whenever she felt like it—a potentially dangerous practice. She taught the porpoise to come out for a reward when she gave a hand signal, and then rarely gave the signal.
C. It is possible to eliminate behavior that is undesirable by bringing it under stimulus control by tying behavior to a signal, and then rarely giving the signal. One trainer successfully used this method to keep an energetic porpoise from coming out of her tank, a potentially dangerous situation. Her trainer taught the porpoise to do it for a reward, in response to a hand signal, and then would rarely give the signal.
D. By using stimulus control, it is possible to eliminate unwanted behavior by tying the behavior to a cue, and then rarely or never give the cue. One trainer was able to use this method to successfully stop a young porpoise from coming out of her tank whenever she felt like it. To curb this potentially dangerous practice, the porpoise was taught by the trainer to come out of the tank for a reward, in response to a hand signal, and then rarely given the signal.

8. I. There is a great deal of concern over the safety of commercial trucks, caused by their greatly increased role in serious accidents since federal deregulation in 1981.
   II. Recently, 60 percent of trucks in New York and Connecticut and 70 percent of trucks in Maryland randomly stopped by state troopers failed safety inspections.
   III. Sixteen states in the United States require no training at all for truck drivers.

8.____

   A. Since federal deregulation in 1981, there has been a great deal of concern over the safety of commercial trucks, and their greatly increased role in serious accidents. Recently, 60 percent of trucks in New York and Connecticut, and 70 percent of trucks in Maryland failed safety inspections. Sixteen states in the United States require no training at all for truck drivers.
   B. There is a great deal of concern over the safety of commercial trucks since federal deregulation in 1981. Their role in serious accidents has greatly increased. Recently, 60 percent of trucks randomly stopped in Connecticut and New York and 70 percent in Maryland failed safety inspections conducted by state troopers. Sixteen states in the United States provide no training at all for truck drivers.
   C. Commercial trucks have a greatly increased role in serious accidents since federal deregulation in 1981. This has led to a great deal of concern.

Recently, 70 percent of trucks in Maryland and 60 percent of trucks in New York and Connecticut failed inspection of those that were randomly stopped by state troopers. Sixteen states in the United States require no training for all truck drivers.

D. Since federal deregulation in 1981, the role that commercial trucks have played in serious accidents has greatly increased, and this has led to a great deal of concern. Recently, 60 percent of trucks in New York and Connecticut, and 70 percent of trucks in Maryland randomly stopped by state troopers failed safety inspections. Sixteen states in the U.S. don't require any training for truck drivers.

9.
I. No matter how much some people have, they still feel unsatisfied and want more, or want to keep what they have forever.
II. One recent television documentary showed several people flying from New York to Paris for a one-day shopping spree to buy platinum earrings, because they were bored.
III. In Brazil, some people were ordering coffins that cost a minimum of $45,000 and are equipping them with deluxe stereos, televisions, and other graveyard necessities.

9.____

A. Some people, despite having a great deal, still feel unsatisfied and want more, or think they can keep what they have forever. One recent documentary on television showed several people enroute from Paris to New York for a one day shopping spree to buy platinum earrings, because they were bored. Some people in Brazil are even ordering coffins equipped with such graveyard necessities as deluxe stereos and televisions. The price of the coffins start at $45,000.
B. No matter how much some people have, they may feel unsatisfied. This leads them to want more, or to want to keep what they have forever. Recently, a television documentary depicting several people flying from New York to Paris for a one day shopping spree to buy platinum earrings. They were bored. Some people in Brazil are ordering coffins that cost at least $45,000 and come equipped with deluxe televisions, stereos and other necessary graveyard items.
C. Some people will be dissatisfied no matter how much they have. They may want more, or they may want to keep what they have forever. One recent television documentary showed several people, motivated by boredom, jetting from New York to Paris for a one-day shopping spree to buy platinum earrings. In Brazil, some people are ordering coffins equipped with deluxe stereos, televisions and other graveyard necessities. The minimum price for these coffins—$45,000.
D. Some people are never satisfied. No matter how much they have they still want more, or think they can keep what they have forever. One television documentary recently showed several people flying from New York to Paris for the day to buy platinum earrings because they were bored. In Brazil, some people are ordering coffins that cost $45,000 and are equipped with deluxe stereos, televisions and other graveyard necessities.

10. I. A television signal or video signal has three parts.
    II. Its parts are the black-and-white portion, the color portion, and the synchronizing (sync) pulses, which keep the picture stable.
    III. Each video source, whether it's a camera or a video-cassette recorder contains its own generator of these synchronizing pulses to accompany the picture that it's sending in order to keep it steady and straight.
    IV. In order to produce a clean recording, a video-cassette recorder must "lock-up" to the sync pulses that are part of the video it is trying to record, and this effort may be very noticeable if the device does not have gunlock.

    A. There are three parts to a television or video signal: the black-and-white part, the color part, and the synchronizing (sync) pulses, which keep the picture stable. Whether it's a video-cassette recorder or a camera, each video source contains its own pulse that synchronizes and generates the picture it's sending in order to keep it straight and steady. A video-cassette recorder must "lock up" to the sync pulses that are part of the video it's trying to record. If the device doesn't have gunlock, this effort must be very noticeable.
    B. A video signal or television is comprised of three parts: the black-and-white portion, the color portion, and the sync (synchronizing) pulses, which keep the picture stable. Whether it's a camera or a video-cassette recorder, each video source contains its own generator of these synchronizing pulses. These accompany the picture that it's sending in order to keep it straight and steady. A video-cassette recorder must "lock up" to the sync pulses that are part of the video it is trying to record in order to produce a clean recording. This effort may be very noticeable if the device does not have gunlock.
    C. There are three parts to a television or video signal: the color portion, the black-and-white portion, and the sync (synchronizing pulses). These keep the picture stable. Each video source, whether it's a video-cassette recorder or a camera, generates these synchronizing pulses accompanying the picture it's sending in order to keep it straight and steady. If a clean recording is to be produced, a video-cassette recorder must store the sync pulses that are part of the video it is trying to record. This effort may not be noticeable if the device does not have gunlock.
    D. A television signal or video signal has three parts: the black-and-white portion, the color portion, and the synchronizing (sync) pulses. It's the sync pulses which keep the picture stable, which accompany it and keep it steady and straight. Whether it's a camera or a video-cassette recorder, each video source contains its own generator of these synchronizing pulses. To produce a clean recording, a video-cassette recorder must "lock up" to the sync pulses that are part of the video it is trying to record. If the device does not have gunlock, this effort may be very noticeable.

10.____

KEY (CORRECT ANSWERS)

1. C
2. B
3. A
4. B
5. D

6. A
7. B
8. D
9. C
10. D

READING COMPREHENSION
UNDERSTANDING AND INTERPRETING WRITTEN MATERIAL
EXAMINATION SECTION
TEST 1

DIRECTIONS: Each question or incomplete statement is followed by several suggested answers or completions. Select the one that BEST answers the question or completes the statement. *PRINT THE LETTER OF THE CORRECT ANSWER IN THE SPACE AT THE RIGHT.*

Questions 1-4.

DIRECTIONS: Questions 1 through 4 are to be answered SOLELY on the basis of the following paragraph.

An annual leave allowance, which combines leaves previously given for vacation, personal business, family illness, and other reasons shall be granted members. Calculation of credits for such leave shall be on an annual basis beginning January 1st of each year. Annual leave credits shall be based on time served by members during preceding calendar year. However, when credits have been accrued and member retires during current year, additional annual leave credits shall, in this instance, be granted at accrual rate of three days for each completed month of service, excluding terminal leave. If accruals granted for completed months of service extend into following month, member shall be granted an additional three days accrual for completed month. This shall be the only condition where accruals in a current year are granted for vacation period in such year.

1. According to the above paragraph, if a fireman's wife were to become seriously ill so that he would take time off from work to be with her, such time off would be deducted from his _____ leave allowance.
   A. annual
   B. vacation
   C. personal business
   D. family illness

2. Terminal leave means leave taken
   A. at the end of the calendar year
   B. at the end of the vacation year
   C. immediately before retirement
   D. before actually earned, because of an emergency

3. A fireman appointed on July 1, 2017 will be able to take his first full or normal annual leave during the period
   A. July 1, 2017 to June 30, 2018
   B. Jan. 1, 2018 to Dec. 31, 2018
   C. July 1, 2018 to June 30, 2019
   D. Jan. 1, 2019 to Dec. 31, 2019

4. According to the above paragraph, a member who retires on July 15 of this year will be entitled to receive leave allowance based on this year of _____ days.
   A. 15
   B. 18
   C. 22
   D. 24

5. Fire alarm boxes are electromechanical devices for transmitting a coded signal. In each box, there is a trainwork of wheels. When the box is operated, a spring-activated code wheel begins to revolve. The code number of the box is etched on the circumference of the code wheel, and the latter is associated with the circuit in such a way that when it revolves it causes the circuit to open and close in a predetermined manner, thereby transmitting its particular signal to the central station. A fire alarm box is nothing more than a device for interrupting the flow of current in a circuit in such a way as to produce a coded signal that may be decoded by the dispatchers in the central office.
Based on the above, select the FALSE statement.
    A. Each standard fire alarm box has its own code wheel.
    B. The code wheel operates when the box is pulled.
    C. The code wheel is operated electrically.
    D. Only the break in the circuit by the notched wheel causes the alarm signal to be transmitted to the central office.

5.____

Questions 6-9.

DIRECTIONS: Questions 6 through 9 are to be answered SOLELY on the basis of the following paragraph.

Ventilation, as used in firefighting operations, means opening up a building or structure in which a fire is burning to release the accumulated heat, smoke, and gases. Lack of knowledge of the principles of ventilation on the part of firemen may result in unnecessary punishment due to ventilation being neglected or improperly handled. While ventilation itself extinguishes no fires, when used in an intelligent manner, it allows firemen to get at the fire more quickly, easily, and with less danger and hardship.

6. According to the above paragraph, the MOST important result of failure to apply the principles of ventilation at a fire may be
    A. loss of public confidence   B. waste of water
    C. excessive use of equipment   D. injury to firemen

6.____

7. It may be inferred from the above paragraph that the CHIEF advantage of ventilation is that it
    A. eliminates the need for gas masks
    B. reduces smoke damage
    C. permits firemen to work closer to the fire
    D. cools the fire

7.____

8. Knowledge of the principles of ventilation, as defined in the above paragraph, would be LEAST important in a fire in a
    A. tenement house   B. grocery store
    C. ship's hold   D. lumberyard

8.____

9. We may conclude from the above paragraph that for the well-trained and equipped fireman, ventilation is
    A. a simple matter   B. rarely necessary
    C. relatively unimportant   D. a basic tool

9.____

Questions 10-13.

DIRECTIONS: Questions 10 through 13 are to be answered SOLELY on the basis of the following passage.

Fire exit drills should be established and held periodically to effectively train personnel to leave their working area promptly upon proper signal and to evacuate the building, speedily but without confusion. All fire exit drills should be carefully planned and carried out in a serious manner under rigid discipline so as to provide positive protection in the event of a real emergency. As a general rule, the local fire department should be furnished advance information regarding the exact date and time the exit drill is scheduled. When it is impossible to hold regular drills, written instructions should be distributed to all employees.

Depending upon individual circumstances, fires in warehouses vary from those of fast development that are almost instantly beyond any possibility of employee control to others of relatively slow development where a small readily attackable flame may be present for periods of time up to 15 minutes or more during which simple attack with fire extinguishers or small building hoses may prevent the fire development. In any case, it is characteristic of many warehouse fires that at a certain point in development they flash up to the top of the stack, increase heat quickly, and spread rapidly. There is a degree of inherent danger in attacking warehouse type fires, and all employees should be thoroughly trained in the use of the types of extinguishers or small hoses in the buildings and well instructed in the necessity of always staying between the fire and a direct pass to an exit.

10. Employees should be instructed that, when fighting a fire, they MUST 10.____
    A. try to control the blaze
    B. extinguish any fire in 15 minutes
    C. remain between the fire and a direct passage to the exit
    D. keep the fire between themselves and the fire exit

11. Whenever conditions are such that regular fire drills cannot be held, then which 11.____
    one of the following actions should be taken?
    A. The local fire department should be notified.
    B. Rigid discipline should be maintained during work hours.
    C. Personnel should be instructed to leave their working area by whatever means are available.
    D. Employees should receive fire drill procedures in writing.

12. The above passage indicates that the purpose of fire exit drills is to train 12.____
    employees to
    A. control a fire before it becomes uncontrollable
    B. act as firefighters
    C. leave the working area promptly
    D. be serious

13. According to the above passage, fire exit drills will prove to be of UTMOST effectiveness if
    A. employee participation is made voluntary
    B. they take place periodically
    C. the fire department actively participates
    D. they are held without advance planning

Questions 14-16.

DIRECTIONS: Questions 14 through 16 are to be answered SOLELY on the basis of the following paragraph.

The heat output from unit heaters will depend on how fast and how completely dry hot steam fills the unit core. For complete and fast air removal and rapid drainage of condensate, use a trap actuated by water or vapor (inverted bucket trap) and not a trap operated by temperature only (thermostatic or bellows trap). A temperature-actuated trap will hold back the hot condensate until it cools to a point where the thermal element opens. When this happens, the condensate backs up in the heater and reduces the heat output. With a water-actuated trap, this will not happen as the water or condensate is discharged as fast as it is formed.

14. On the basis of the information given in the above paragraph, it can be concluded that the PROPER type of trap to use for a unit heater is a(n) _____ trap.
    A. thermostatic
    B. bellows-type
    C. inverted bucket
    D. temperature

15. According to the above paragraph, the MAIN reason for using the type of trap specified for a unit heater is to
    A. bring the condensate up to steam temperature
    B. prevent reduction in the heat output of the unit heater
    C. permit cycling of the heater
    D. maintain constant temperature of condensate in the trap

16. As used in the above paragraph, the word *actuated* means MOST NEARLY
    A. clogged   B. operated   C. cleaned   D. vented

Questions 17-25.

DIRECTIONS: Questions 17 through 25 are to be answered SOLELY on the basis of the following passage. Each question consists of a statement. You are to indicate whether the statement is TRUE (T) or FALSE (F).

MOVING AN OFFICE

An office with all its equipment is sometimes moved during working hours. This is a difficult task and must be done in an orderly manner to avoid confusion. The operation should be planned in such a way as not to interrupt the progress of work usually done in the office and to make possible the accurate placement of the furniture and records in the new location. If the office moves to a place inside the same building, the desks and files are moved with all their contents. If the movement is to another building, the contents of each desk and file are placed in boxes. Each box is marked with a letter showing the particular section in the new quarters to which it is to be moved. Also marked on each box is the number of the desk or file on which the box is to be placed. Each piece of equipment must have a numbered tag. The number of each piece of equipment is put in soft chalk on the floor in the new office to show the proper location, and several floor plans are made to show where each piece of equipment goes. When the moving is done, someone is stationed at each of the several exits of the old office to see that each box or piece of equipment has its destination clearly marked on it. At the new office, someone stands at each of the several entrances with a copy of the floor plan and directs the placing of the furniture and equipment according to the floor plan. No one should interfere at this point with the arrangements shown on the plan. Improvements in arrangement can be considered and made at a later date.

17. It is a hard job to move an office from one place to another during working hours. 17.____

18. Confusion cannot be avoided if an office is moved during working hours. 18.____

19. The work usually done in an office must be stopped for the day when the office is moved during working hours. 19.____

20. If an office is moved from one floor to another in the same building, the contents of a desk are taken out and put into boxes for moving. 20.____

21. If boxes are used to hold material from desks when moving an office, the box is numbered the same as the desk on which it is to be put. 21.____

22. Letters are marked in soft chalk on the floor at the new quarters to show where the desks should go when moved. 22.____

23. When the moving begins, a person is put at each exit of the old office to check that each box and piece of equipment has clearly marked on it where to go. 23.____

24. A person stationed at each entrance of the new quarters to direct the placing of the furniture and equipment has a copy of the floor plan of the new quarters. 24.____

25. If, while the furniture is being moved into the new office, a person helping at a doorway gets an idea of a better way to arrange the furniture, he should change the planned arrangement and make a record of the change. 25.____

KEY (CORRECT ANSWERS)

1.	A	11.	D
2.	C	12.	C
3.	D	13.	B
4.	B	14.	C
5.	C	15.	B
6.	D	16.	B
7.	C	17.	T
8.	D	18.	F
9.	D	19.	F
10.	C	20.	F

21. T
22. F
23. T
24. T
25. F

TEST 2

DIRECTIONS: Each question or incomplete statement is followed by several suggested answers or completions. Select the one that BEST answers the question or completes the statement. *PRINT THE LETTER OF THE CORRECT ANSWER IN THE SPACE AT THE RIGHT.*

Questions 1-4.

DIRECTIONS: Questions 1 through 4 are to be answered SOLELY on the basis of the following paragraph.

In all cases of homicide, members of the Police Department who investigate will make every effort to obtain statements from dying persons. Such statements are of the greatest importance to the District Attorney. In many cases, there may be a failure to solve the crime if they are not taken. The principal element to be considered in taking the declaration of a dying person is his mental attitude. In order to be admissible in evidence, the person must have no hope of recovery. The patient will be fully interrogated on that point before a statement is taken.

1. In cases of homicide, according to the above paragraph, members of the police force will
    A. try to change the mental attitude of the dying person
    B. attempt to obtain a statement from the dying person
    C. not give the information they obtain directly to the District Attorney
    D. be careful not to injure the dying person unnecessarily

2. The mental attitude of the person making the dying statement is of GREAT importance because it can determine, according to the above paragraph, whether the
    A. victim should be interrogated in the presence of witnesses
    B. victim will be willing to make a statement of any kind
    C. statement will tell the District Attorney who committed the crime
    D. the statement can be used as evidence

3. District Attorneys find that statements of a dying person are important, according to the above paragraph, because
    A. it may be that the victim will recover and then refuse to testify
    B. they are important elements in determining the mental attitude of the victim
    C. they present a point of view
    D. it may be impossible to punish the criminal without such a statement

4. A well-known gangster is found dying from a bullet wound. The patrolman first on the scene, in the presence of witnesses, tells the man that he is going to die and asks, *Who shot you?* The gangster says, *Jones shot me, but he hasn't killed me. I'll live to get him.* He then falls back dead.
According to the above paragraph, this statement is
    A. *admissible* in evidence; the man was obviously speaking the truth
    B. *not admissible* in evidence; the man obviously did not believe that he was dying

C. *admissible* in evidence; there were witnesses to the statement
D. *not admissible* in evidence; the victim did not sign any statement and the evidence is merely hearsay

Questions 5-7.

DIRECTIONS: Questions 5 through 7 are to be answered SOLELY on the basis of the following paragraph.

The factors contributing to crime and delinquency are varied and complex. The home and its immediate environment have been found to be crucial in determining the behavior patterns of the individual, and criminality can frequently be traced to faulty family relationships and a bad neighborhood. But in the search for a clearer understanding of the underlying causes of delinquent and criminal behavior, the total environment must be taken into consideration.

5. According to the above paragraph, family relationships   5.____
   A. tend to become faulty in bad neighborhoods
   B. are important in determining the actions of honest people as well as criminals
   C. are the only important element in the understanding of causes of delinquency
   D. are determined by the total environment

6. According to the above paragraph, the causes of crime and delinquency are   6.____
   A. not simple   B. not meaningless
   C. meaningless   D. simple

7. According to the above paragraph, faulty family relationships FREQUENTLY are   7.____
   A. responsible for varied and complex results
   B. caused when one or both parents have a criminal behavior pattern
   C. independent of the total environment
   D. the cause of criminal acts

Questions 8-10.

DIRECTIONS: Questions 8 through 10 are to be answered SOLELY on the basis of the following paragraph.

A change in the specific problems which confront the police and in the methods for dealing with them has taken place in the last few decades. The automobile is a two-way symbol of this change in policing. It menaces every city with a complicated traffic problem and has speeded up the process of committing a crime and making a getaway, but at the same time has increased the effectiveness of police operations. However, the major concern of police departments continues to be the antisocial or criminal actions and behavior of human beings.

8. On the basis of the above paragraph, it can be stated that, for the most part, in the past few decades the specific problems of a police force
   A. have changed but the general problems have not
   B. as well as the general problems have changed
   C. have remained the same but the general problems have changed
   D. as well as the general problems have remained the same

8.____

9. According to the above paragraph, advances in science and industry have, in general, made the police
   A. operations less effective from the overall point of view
   B. operations more effective from the overall point of view
   C. abandon older methods of solving police problems
   D. concern themselves more with the antisocial acts of human beings

9.____

10. The automobile is a *two-way symbol*, according to the above paragraph, because its use
    A. has speeded up getting to and away from the scene of a crime
    B. both helps and hurts police operations
    C. introduces a new antisocial act—traffic violation—and does away with criminals like horse thieves
    D. both increases and decreases speed by introducing traffic problems

10.____

Questions 11-14.

DIRECTIONS: Questions 11 through 14 are to be answered SOLELY on the basis of the following passage on INSTRUCTIONS TO COIN AND TOKEN CASHIERS.

INSTRUCTIONS TO COIN AND TOKEN CASHIERS

Cashiers should reset the machine registers to an even starting number before commencing the day's work. Money bags received directly from collecting agents shall be counted and receipted for on the collecting agent's form. Each cashier shall be responsible for all coin or token bags accepted by him. He must examine all bags to be used for bank deposits for cuts and holes before placing them in use. Care must be exercised so that bags are not cut in opening them. Each bag must be opened separately and verified before another bag is opened. The machine register must be cleared before starting the count of another bag. The amount shown on the machine register must be compared with the amount on the bag tag. The empty bag must be kept on the table for re-examination should there be a difference between the amount on the bag tag and the amount on the machine register.

11. A cashier should BEGIN his day's assignment by
    A. counting and accepting all money bags
    B. resetting the counting machine register
    C. examining all bags for cuts and holes
    D. verifying the contents of all money bags

11.____

12. In verifying the amount of money in the bags received from the collecting agent, it is BEST to
    A. check the amount in one bag at a time
    B. base the total on the amount on the collecting agent's form
    C. repeat the total shown on the bag tag
    D. refer to the bank deposit receipt

12.____

13. A cashier is instructed to keep each empty coin bag on his table while verifying its contents CHIEFLY because, as long as the bag is on the table
    A. it cannot be misplaced
    B. the supervisor can see how quickly the cashier works
    C. cuts and holes are easily noticed
    D. a recheck is possible in case the machine count disagrees with the bag tag total

13.____

14. The INSTRUCTIONS indicate that it is NOT proper procedure for a cashier to
    A. assume that coin bags are free of cuts and holes
    B. compare the machine register total with the total shown on the bag tag
    C. sign a form when he receives coin bags
    D. reset the machine register before starting the day's counting

14.____

Questions 15-17.

DIRECTIONS: Questions 15 through 17 are to be answered SOLELY on the basis of the following passage.

The mass media are an integral part of the daily life of virtually every American. Among these media the youngest, television, is the most pervasive. Ninety-five percent of American homes have at least one T.V. set, and on the average that set is in use for about 40 hours each week. The central place of television in American life makes this medium the focal point of a growing national concern over the effects of media portrayals of violence on the values, attitudes, and behavior of an ever-increasing audience.

In our concern about violence and its causes, it is easy to make television a scapegoat. But we emphasize the fact that there is no simple answer to the problem of violence—no single explanation of its causes, and no single prescription for its control. It should be remembered that America also experienced high levels of crime and violence in periods before the advent of television.

The problem of balance, taste and artistic merit in entertaining programs on television are complex. We cannot <u>countenance</u> government censorship of television. Nor would we seek to impose arbitrary limitations on programming which might jeopardize television's ability to deal in dramatic presentations with controversial social issues. Nonetheless, we are deeply troubled by television's constant portrayal of violence, not in any genuine attempt to focus artistic expression on the human condition, but rather in pandering to a public preoccupation with violence that television itself has helped to generate,

15. According to the above passage, television uses violence MAINLY
    A. to highlight the reality of everyday existence
    B. to satisfy the audience's hunger for destructive action

15.____

C. to shape the values and attitudes of the public
D. when it films documentaries concerning human conflict

16. Which one of the following statements is BEST supported by the above passage? 16._____
    A. Early American history reveals a crime pattern which is not related to television.
    B. Programs should give presentations of social issues and never portray violent acts.
    C. Television has proven that entertainment programs can easily make the balance between taste and artistic merit a simple matter.
    D. Values and behavior should be regulated by governmental censorship.

17. Of the following, which word has the same meaning as *countenance*, as used in the above passage? 17._____
    A. Approve   B. Exhibit   C. Oppose   D. Reject

Questions 18-21.

DIRECTIONS: Questions 18 through 21 are to be answered SOLELY on the basis of the following passage.

   Maintenance of leased or licensed areas on public parks or land has always been a problem. A good rule to follow in the administration and maintenance of such areas is to limit the responsibility of any lessee or licensee to the maintenance of the structures and grounds essential to the efficient operation of the concession, not including areas for the general use of the public, such as picnic areas, public comfort stations, etc.; except where such facilities are leased to another public agency or where special conditions make such inclusion practicable, and where a good standard of maintenance can be assured and enforced. If local conditions and requirements are such that public use areas are included, adequate safeguards to the public should be written into contracts and enforced in their administration, to insure that maintenance by the concessionaire shall be equal to the maintenance standards for other park property.

18. According to the above passage, when an area on a public park is leased to a concessionaire, it is usually BEST to 18._____
    A. confine the responsibility of the concessionaire to operation of the facilities and leave the maintenance function to the park agency
    B. exclude areas of general public use from the maintenance obligation of the concessionaire
    C. make the concessionaire responsible for maintenance of the entire area including areas of general public use
    D. provide additional comfort station facilities for the area

19. According to the above passage, a valid reason for giving a concessionaire responsibility for maintenance of a picnic area within his leased area is that 19._____
    A. local conditions and requirements make it practicable
    B. more than half of the picnic area falls within his leased area
    C. the concessionaire has leased picnic facilities to another public agency
    D. the picnic area falls entirely within his leased area

117

20. According to the above passage, a precaution that should be taken when a concessionaire is made responsible for maintenance of an area of general public use in a park is
    A. making sure that another public agency has not previously been made responsible for this area
    B. providing the concessionaire with up-to-date equipment, if practicable
    C. requiring that the concessionaire take out adequate insurance for the protection of the public
    D. writing safeguards to the public into the contract

20.____

KEY (CORRECT ANSWERS)

1.	B	11.	B
2.	D	12.	A
3.	D	13.	D
4.	B	14.	A
5.	B	15.	B
6.	A	16.	A
7.	D	17.	A
8.	A	18.	B
9.	B	19.	A
10.	B	20.	D

TEST 3

DIRECTIONS: Each question or incomplete statement is followed by several suggested answers or completions. Select the one that BEST answers the question or completes the statement. *PRINT THE LETTER OF THE CORRECT ANSWER IN THE SPACE AT THE RIGHT.*

Questions 1-5.

DIRECTIONS: Questions 1 through 5 are to be answered SOLELY on the basis of the following paragraph.

    Physical inspections are an important tool for the examiner because he will have to decide the case in many instances on the basis of the inspection report. Most proceedings in a rent office are commenced by the filing of a written application or complaint by an interested party; that is, either the landlord or the tenant. Such an application or complaint must be filed in duplicate in order that the opposing party may be served with a copy of the application or complaint and thus be given an opportunity to answer and oppose it. Sometimes, a further opportunity is given the applicant to file a written rebuttal or reply to his adversary's answer. Often an examiner can make a determination or decision based on the written application, the answer, and the reply to the answer; and, of course, it would speed up operations if it were always possible to make decisions based on written documents only. Unfortunately, decisions can't always be made that way. There are numerous occasions where <u>disputed</u> issues of fact remain which cannot be <u>resolved</u> on the basis of the written statements of the parties. Typical examples are the following: The tenant claims that the refrigerator or stove or bathroom fixture is not functioning properly and the landlord denies this It is obvious that in such cases an inspection of the accommodations is almost the only means of resolving such disputed issues,

1. According to the above paragraph,   1.____
   A. physical inspections are made in all cases
   B. physical inspections are seldom made
   C. it is sometimes possible to determine the facts in a case without a physical inspection
   D. physical inspections are made when it is necessary to verify the examiner's determination

2. According to the above paragraph, in MOST cases, proceedings are started by a(n)   2.____
   A. inspector discovering a violation
   B. oral complaint by a tenant or landlord
   C. request from another agency, such as the Building Department
   D. written complaint by a tenant or landlord

3. According to the above paragraph, when a tenant files an application with the rent office, the landlord is   3.____
   A. not told about the proceeding until after the examiner makes his determination
   B. given the duplicate copy of the application

C. notified by means of an inspector visiting the premises
D. not told about the proceeding until after the inspector has visited the premises

4. As used in the above paragraph, the word *disputed* means MOST NEARLY   4._____
   A. unsettled   B. contested   C. definite   D. difficult

5. As used in the above paragraph, the word *resolved* means MOST NEARLY   5._____
   A. settled   B. fixed   C. helped   D. amended

Questions 6-10.

DIRECTIONS: Questions 6 through 10 are to be answered SOLELY on the basis of the following paragraph.

The examiner should order or request an inspection of the housing accommodations. His request for a physical inspection should be in writing, identify the accommodations and the landlord and the tenant, and specify precisely just what the inspector is to look for and report on. Unless this request is specific and lists in detail every item which the examiner wishes to be reported, the examiner will find that the inspection has not served its purpose and that even with the inspector's report, he is still in no position to decide the case due to loose ends which have not been completely tied up. The items that the examiner is interested in should be separately numbered on the inspection request and the same number referred to in the inspector's report. You can see what it would mean if an inspector came back with a report that did not cover everything. It may mean a tremendous waste of time and often require a re-inspection.

6. According to the above paragraph, the inspector makes an inspection on the order of   6._____
   A. the landlord   B. the tenant
   C. the examiner   D. both the landlord and the tenant

7. According to the above paragraph, the reason for numbering each item that an inspector reports on is so that   7._____
   A. the report is neat
   B. the report can be easily read and referred to
   C. none of the examiner's requests for information is missed
   D. the report will be specific

8. The one of the following items that is NOT necessarily included in the request for inspection is   8._____
   A. location of dwelling   B. name of landlord
   C. item to be checked   D. type of building

9. As used in the above paragraph, the word *precisely* means MOST NEARLY   9._____
   A. exactly   B. generally   C. usually   D. strongly

10. As used in the above paragraph, the words *in detail* mean MOST NEARLY   10._____
    A. clearly   B. item by item   C. substantially   D. completely

Questions 11-13.

DIRECTIONS: Questions 11 through 13 are to be answered SOLELY on the basis of the following passage.

The agreement under which a tenant rents property from a landlord is known as a lease. Generally speaking, leases are classified as either short-term or long-term in duration. They are further subdivided according to the method used to determine the amount of periodic rent payments. Of the following types of lease in use, the more commonly used ones are the following:
1. The straight or fixed lease is one in which rent may be paid in equal amounts throughout the duration of the lease. These are usually restricted to short-term leasing, or somewhat longer-term if clauses in the lease provide for periodic escalation of payments as the economy shifts.
2. Percentage leasing, used for short-term commercial leasing, provides the landlord with a stipulated percentage of a tenant's gross sales from goods and services sold on the premises, in addition to a fixed amount of rent.
3. The net lease, generally long-term (ten years or more), requires the tenant to pay all operating costs, including real estate taxes and insurance. In a net-net lease, the tenant further agrees to meet mortgage interest and principal payments.
4. An escalated lease, which is a long-term lease, requires rent to be of a stipulated base amount which periodically is subject to escalation in accordance with cost-of-living index scales, or in direct proportion to taxes, insurance, and operating costs.

11. Based on the information given in the passage, which type of lease is MOST likely to be advantageous to a landlord if there is a high rate of inflation? _____ lease.
    A. Fixed   B. Percentage   C. Net   D. Escalated

11.____

12. On the basis of thee above passage, which types of lease would generally be MOST suitable for a well-established textile company which requires permanent facilities for its large operations?
    _____ lease and _____ lease.
    A. Percentage; escalated   B. Escalated; net
    C. Straight; net   D. Straight; percentage

12.____

13. According to the above passage, the ONLY type of lease which assures the same amount of rent throughout a specified interval is the _____ lease.
    A. straight   B. percentage   C. net-net   D. escalated

13.____

Questions 14-15.

DIRECTIONS: Questions 14 and 15 are to be answered SOLELY on the basis of the following passage.

If you like people, if you seek contact with them rather than hide yourself in a corner, if you study your fellow men sympathetically, if you try consistently to contribute something to their success and happiness, if you are reasonably generous with your thought and your time, if you have a partial reserve with everyone but a seeming reserve with no one, you will get along with your superiors, your subordinates, and the human race.

By the scores of thousands, precepts and platitudes have been written for the guidance of personal conduct. The odd part of it is that, despite all of this labor, most of the frictions in modern society arise from the individual's feeling of inferiority, his false pride, his vanity, his unwillingness to yield space to any other man and his consequent urge to throw his own weight around. Goethe said that the quality which best enables a man to renew his own life, in his relation to others, is his capability of renouncing particular things at the right moment in order warmly to embrace something new in the next.

14. On the basis of the above passage, it may be INFERRED that
    A. a person should be unwilling to renounce privileges
    B. a person should realize that loss of a desirable job assignment may come at an opportune moment
    C. it is advisable for a person to maintain a considerable amount of reserve in his relationship with unfamiliar people
    D. people should be ready to contribute generously to a worthy charity

15. Of the following, the MOST valid implication made by the above passage is that
    A. a wealthy person who spends a considerable amount of money entertaining his friends is not really getting along with them
    B. if a person studies his fellow men carefully and impartially, he will tend to have good relationships with them
    C. individuals who maintain seemingly little reserve in their relationships with people have in some measure overcome their own feelings of inferiority
    D. most precepts that have been written for the guidance of personal conduct in relationships with other people are invalid

Questions 16-17.

DIRECTIONS: Questions 16 and 17 are to be answered SOLELY on the basis of the following passage.

When a design for a new bank note of the Federal Government has been prepared by the Bureau of Engraving and Printing and has been approved by the Secretary of the Treasury, the engravers begin the work of cutting the design in steel. No one engraver does all the work. Each man is a specialist. One works only on portraits, another on lettering, another on scroll work, and so on. Each engraver, with a steel tool known as a graver, and aided by a powerful magnifying glass, carefully carves his portion of the design into the steel. He knows that one false cut or a slip of his tool, or one miscalculation of width or depth of line, may destroy the merit of his work. A single mistake means that months or weeks of labor will have been in vain. The bureau is proud of the fact that no counterfeiter ever has duplicated the excellent work of its expert engravers.

16. According to the above passage, each engraver in the Bureau of Engraving and Printing
    A. must be approved by the Secretary of the Treasury before he can begin work on the design for a new bank note
    B. is responsible for engraving a complete design of a new bank note by himself
    C. designs new bank notes and submits them for approval to the Secretary of the Treasury
    D. performs sonly a specific part of the work of engraving a design for a new bank note

16.____

17. According to the above passage,
    A. an engraver's tools are not available to a counterfeiter
    B. mistakes made in engraving a design can be corrected immediately with little delay in the work of the Bureau
    C. the skilled work of the engravers has not been successfully reproduced by counterfeiter
    D. careful carving and cutting by the engraver is essential to prevent damage to equipment

17.____

Questions 18-21.

DIRECTIONS: Questions 18 through 21 are to be answered SOLELY on the basis of the following passage.

In the late fifties, the average American housewife spent $4.50 per day for a family of four on food and 5.15 hours in food preparation, if all of her food was *home prepared*; she spent $5.80 per day and 3.245 hours if all of her food was purchased *partially prepared*; and $6.70 per day and 1.64 hours if all of her food was purchased *ready-to-serve*.

Americans spent about 20 billion dollars for food products in 1941. They spent nearly 70 billion dollars in 1958. They spent 25 percent of their cash income on food in 1958. For the same kinds and quantities of food that consumers bought in 1941, they would have spent only 16% of their cash income in 1958. It is obvious that our food does cost more. Many factors contribute to this increase besides the additional cost that might be attributed to processing. Consumption of more expensive food items, higher marketing margins, and more food eaten in restaurants are other factors.

The Census of Manufacturers gives some indication of the total bill for processing. The value added by manufacturing of food and kindred products amounted to 3.5 billion of the 20 billion dollars spent for food in 1941. In the year 1958, the comparable figure had climbed to 14 billion dollars.

18. According to the above passage, the cash income of Americans in 1958 was MOST NEARLY _____ billion dollars.
    A. 11.2   B. 17.5   C. 70   D. 280

18.____

19. According to the above passage, if Americans bought the same kinds and quantities of food in 1958 as they did in 1941, they would have spent MOST NEARLY _____ billion dollars.
    A. 20   B. 45   C. 74   D. 84

19.____

20. According to the above passage, the percent increase in money spent for food in 1958 over 1941, as compared with the percentage increase in money spent for food processing in the same years,
    A. was greater
    B. was less
    C. was the same
    D. cannot be determined from the passage

21. In 1958, an American housewife who bought all of her food ready-to-serve saved time, as compared with the housewife who prepared all of her food at home
    A. 1.6 hours daily
    B. 1.9 hours daily
    C. 3.5 hours daily
    D. an amount of time which cannot be determined from the above passage

Questions 22-25.

DIRECTIONS: Questions 22 through 25 are to be answered SOLELY on the basis of the following passage.

Any member of the retirement system who is in city service, who files a proper application for service credit and agrees to deductions from his compensation at triple his normal rate of contribution, shall be credited with a period of city service previous to the beginning of his present membership in the retirement system. The period of service credited shall be equal to the period throughout which such triple deductions are made, but may not exceed the total of the city service the number rendered between his first day of eligibility for membership in the retirement system and the day he last became a member. After triple contributions for all of the first three years of service credit claimed, the remaining service credit may be purchased by a single payment of the sum of the remaining payments. If the total time purchasable exceeds ten years, triple contributions may be made for one-half of such time, and the remaining time purchased by a single payment of the sum of the remaining payments. Credit for service acquired in the above manner may be used only in determining the amount of any retirement benefit. Eligibility for such benefit will, in all cases, be based upon service rendered after the employee's membership last began, and will be exclusive of service credit purchased as described above.

22. According to the above passage, in order to obtain credit for city service previous to the beginning of an employee's present membership in the retirement system, the employee must
    A. apply for the service credit and consent to additional contributions to the retirement system
    B. apply for the service credit before he renews his membership in the retirement system
    C. have previous city service which does not exceed ten years
    D. make contributions to the retirement system for three years

23. According to the information in the above passage, credit for city service previous to the beginning of an employee's present membership in the retirement system is
    A. credited up to a maximum of ten years
    B. credited to any member of the retirement system
    C. used in determining the amount of the employee's benefits
    D. used in establishing the employee's eligibility to receive benefits

23.____

24. According to the information in the above passage, a member of the retirement system may purchase service credit for
    A. the period of time between his first day of eligibility for membership in the retirement system and the date he applies for the service credit
    B. one-half of the total of his previous city service if the total time exceeds ten years
    C. the period of time throughout which triple deductions are made
    D. the period of city service between his first day of eligibility for membership in the retirement system and the day he last became a member

24.____

25. Suppose that a member of the retirement system has filed an application for service credit for five years of previous city service.
    Based on the information in the above passage, the employee may purchase credit for this previous city service by making
    A. triple contributions for three years
    B. triple contributions for one-half of the time and a single payment of the sum of the remaining payments
    C. triple contributions for three years and a single payment of the sum of the remaining payments
    D. a single payment of the sum of the payments

25.____

KEY (CORRECT ANSWERS)

1.	C	11.	D
2.	D	12.	B
3.	B	13.	A
4.	B	14.	B
5.	A	15.	C
6.	C	16.	D
7.	C	17.	C
8.	D	18.	D
9.	A	19.	B
10.	B	20.	B

21.	C
22.	A
23.	C
24.	D
25.	C

BASIC FUNDAMENTALS OF A FINANCIAL STATEMENT

TABLE OF CONTENTS

	PAGE
Commentary	1
Financial Reports	1
Balance Sheet	1
Assets	1
The ABC Manufacturing Co., Inc.	
Consolidated Balance Sheet – December 31	2
Fixed Assets	3
Depreciation	4
Intangibles	4
Liabilities	5
Reserves	6
Capital Stock	6
Surplus	6
What Does the Balance Sheet Show?	7
Net Working Capital	7
Inventory and Inventory Turnover	8
Net Book Value of Securities	8
Proportion of Bonds, Preferred and Common Stock	9
The Income Account	10
Cost of Sales	11
The ABC Manufacturing Co., Inc.	
Consolidated Income and Earned Surplus – December 31	11
Maintenance	12
Interest Charges	13
Net Income	13
Analyzing the Income Account	14
Interest Coverage	15
Earnings Per Common Share	15
Stock Prices	16
Important Terms and Concepts	17

BASIC FUNDAMENTALS OF A FINANCIAL STATEMENT

COMMENTARY

The ability to read and understand a financial statement is a basic requirement for the accountant, auditor, account clerk, bookkeeper, bank examiner, budget examiner, and, of course, for the executive who must manage and administer departmental affairs.

FINANCIAL REPORTS

Are financial reports really as difficult as all that? Well, if you know they are not so difficult because you have worked with them before, this section will be of auxiliary help for you. However, if you find financial statements a bit murky, but realize their great importance to you, we ought to get along fine together. For "mathematics," all we'll use is fourth-grade arithmetic.

Accountants, like all other professionals, have developed a specialized vocabulary. Sometimes this is helpful and sometimes plain confusing (like their practice of calling the income account, "Statement of Profit and Loss," when it is bound to be one or the other). But there are really only a score or so technical terms that you will have to get straight in mind. After that is done, the whole foggy business will begin to clear and in no time at all you'll be able to talk as wisely as the next fellow.

BALANCE SHEET

Look at the sample balance sheet printed on Page 2, and we'll have an insight into how it is put together. This particular report is neither the simplest that could be issued, nor the most complicated. It is a good average sample of the kind of report issues by an up-to-date manufacturing company.

Note particularly that the balance sheet represents the situation as it stood on one particular day, December 31, not the record of a year's operation. This balance sheet is broken into two parts on the left are shown *ASSETS* and on the right *LIABILITIES*. Under the asset column, you will find listed the value of things the company owns or are owed to the company. Under liabilities are listed the things the company owes to others, plus reserves, surplus, and the stated value of the stockholders' interest in the company.

One frequently hears the comment, "Well, I don't see what a good balance sheet is anyway, because the assets and liabilities are always the same whether the company is successful or not."

It is true that they always balance and, by itself, a balance sheet doesn't tell much until it is analyzed. Fortunately, we can make a balance sheet tell its story without too much effort—often an extremely revealing story, particularly, if we compare the records of several years.

ASSETS

The first notation on the asset side of the balance sheet is *CURRENT ASSETS* (Item 1). In general, current assets include cash and things that can be turned into cash in a hurry, or that, in the normal course of business, will be turned into cash in the reasonably near future, usually within a year.

Item 2 on our sample sheet is *CASH*. Cash is just what you would expect—bills and silver in the till and money on deposit in the bank.

UNITED STATES GOVERNMENT SECURITIES is Item 3. The general practice is to show securities listed as current assets at cost or market value, whichever is lower. The figure, for all reasonable purposes, represents the amount by which total cash could be easily increased if the company wanted to sell these securities.

The next entry is *ACCOUNTS RECEIVABLE* (Item 4). Here we find the total amount of money owed to the company by its regular business creditors and collectable within the next year. Most of the money is owed to the company by its customers for goods that the company delivered on credit. If this were a department store instead of a manufacturer, what you owed the store on our charge account would be included here. Because some people fail to pay their bills, the company sets up a reserve for doubtful accounts, which it subtracts from all the money owed.

THE ABC MANUFACTURING COMPANY, INC.
CONSOLIDATED BALANCE SHEET – DECEMBER 31

Item			Item		
1. CURRENT ASSETS			16. CURRENT LIABILITIES		
2. Cash			17. Accts. Payable		$300,000
3. U.S. Government Securities			18. Accrued Taxes		800,000
4. Accounts Receivable (less reserves)		2,000,000	19. Accrued Wages, interest and Other Expenses		370,000
5. Inventories (at lower of cost or market)		2,000,000	20. Total Current Liabilities		$1,470,000
6. Total Current Assets		$7,000,000	21. FIRST MORTGAGE SINKING FUND BONDS, 3½ % DUE 2020		$2,000,000
7. INVESTMENT IN AFFILIATED COMPANY Not consolidated (at cost, not in excess of net assets)		200,000	22. RESERVE FOR CONTINGENCIES		200,000
8. OTHER INVESTMENTS At cost, less than market		100,000	23. CAPITAL STOCK: 24. 5% Preferred Stock (authorized and issued 10,000 shares of $100 par shares of $100 (par value)	$1,000,000	
9. PLANT IMPROVEMENT FUND		550,000			
10. PROPERTY, PLANT AND EQUIPMENT: Cost	$8,000,000		25. Common stock (authorized and issued 400,000 shares of no par value)	1,000,000	
11. Less Reserve for Depreciation	5,000,000				
12. NET PROPERTY		3,000,000			2,000,000
13. PREPAYMENTS		50,000	26. SURPLUS:		
14. DEFERRED CHARGES		100,000	27. Earned	3,530,000	
15. PATENTS AND GOODWILL		100,000	28. Capital (arising from sale of common capital stock at price in excess of stated value)	1,900,000	
					5,430,000
TOTAL		$11,000,000	TOTAL		$11,100,000

Item 5, *INVENTORIES*, is the value the company places on the supplies it owns. The inventory of a manufacturer may contain raw materials that it uses in making the things it sells, partially finished goods in process of manufacture, and, finally, completed merchandise that it is ready to sell. Several methods are used to arrive at the value placed on these various items. The most common is to value them at their cost or present market value, whichever is lower.

You can be reasonably confident, however, that the figure given is an honest and significant one for the particular industry if the report is certified by a reputable firm of public accountants.

Next on the asset side is *TOTAL CURRENT ASSETS* (Item 6). This is an extremely important figure when used in connection with other items in the report, which we will come to presently. Then we will discover how to make total current assets tell their story.

INVESTMENT IN AFFILIATED COMPANY Item 7) represents the cost to our parent company of the capital stock of its subsidiary or affiliated company. A subsidiary is simply one company that is controlled by another. Most corporations that own other companies outright lump the figures in a CONSOLIDATED BALANCE SHEET. This means that, under cash, for example, one would find a total figure that represented all of the cash of the parent company and of its wholly owned subsidiary. This is a perfectly reasonable procedure because, in the last analysis, all of the money is controlled by the same persons.

Our typical company shows that it has *OTHER INVESTMENTS* (Item 8), in addition to its affiliated company. Sometimes good marketable securities other than Government bonds are carried as current assets, but the more conservative practice is to list these other security holdings separately. If they have been bought as a permanent investment, they would always be shown by themselves. "At cost, less than market" means that our company paid $100,000 for these other investments, but they are now worth more.

Among our assets is a *PLANT IMPROVEMENT FUND* (Item 9). Of course, this item does not appear in all company balance sheets, but is typical of special funds that companies set up for one purpose or another. For example, money set aside to pay off part of the bonded debt of a company might be segregated into a special fund. The money our directors have put aside to improve the plant would often be invested in Government bonds,

FIXED ASSETS

The next item (10) is *PROPERTY, PLANT, AND EQUIPMENT*, but it might just as well be labeled Fixed Assets as these items are used more or less interchangeably, Under Item 10, the report gives the value of land, buildings, and machinery and such movable things as trucks, furniture, and hand tools. Historically, probably more sins were committed against this balance sheet item than any other.

In olden days, cattlemen used to drive their stock to market in the city. It was a common trick to stop outside of town, spread out some salt for the cattle to make them thirsty and then let them drink all the water they could hold. When they were weighed for sale, the cattlemen would collect cash for the water the stock had drunk. Business buccaneers, taking the cue from their farmer friends, would often "write up" the value of their fixed assets. In other words, they would increase the value shown on the balance sheet, making the capital stock appear to be worth a lot more than it was. *Watered stock* proved a bad investment for most stockholders. The practice has, fortunately, been stopped, though it took major financial reorganizations to squeeze the water out of some securities.

The most common practice today is to list fixed assets at cost. Often, there is no ready market for most of the things that fall under this heading, so it is not possible to give market value. A good report will tell what is included under fixed assets and how it has been valued. If the value has been increased by *write-up* or decreased by *write-down*, a footnote explanation is usually given. A *write-up* might occur, for instance, if the value of real estate increased substantially. A *write-down* might follow the invention of a new machine that put an important part of the company's equipment out of date.

DEPRECIATION

Naturally, all of the fixed property of a company will wear out in time (except, of course, non-agricultural land). In recognition of this fact, companies set up a *RESERVE FOR APPRECIATION* (Item 11). If a truck costs $4,000 and is expected to last four years, it will be depreciated at the rate of $1,000 a year.

Two other items also frequently occur in connection with depreciation—*depletion* and *obsolescence*. Companies may lump depreciation, depletion, and obsolescence under a single title, or list them separately.

Depletion is a term used primarily by mining and oil companies (or any of the so-called extractive industries). Depletion means exhaust or use up. As the oil or other natural resource is used up, a reserve is set up, to compensate for the natural wealth the company no longer owns. This reserve is set up in recognition of the fact that, as the company sells its natural product, it must get back not only the cost of extracting but also the original cost of the natural resource.

Obsolescence represents the loss in value because a piece of property has gone out of date before it wore out. Airplanes are modern examples of assets that tend to get behind the times long before the parts wear out. (Women and husbands will be familiar with the speed at which ladies' hats "obsolesce.")

In our sample balance sheet we have placed the reserve for depreciation under fixed assets and then subtracted, giving us *NET PROPERTY* (Item 12), which we add into the asset column. Sometimes, companies put the reserve for depreciation in the liability column. As you can see, the effect is just the same whether it is *subtracted* from assets or *added* to liabilities.

The manufacturer, whose balance sheet we use, rents a New York showroom and pays his rent yearly, in advance. Consequently, he has listed under assets *PREPAYMENTS* (Item 13). This is listed as an asset because he has paid for the use of the showroom, but has not yet received the benefit from its use. The use is something coming to the firm in the following year and, hence, is an asset. The dollar value of this asset will decrease by one-twelfth each month during the coming year.

DEFERRED CHARGES (Item 14) represents a type of expenditure similar to prepayment. For example, our manufacturer brought out a new product last year, spending $100,000 introducing it to the market. As the benefit from this expenditure will be returned over months or even years to come, the manufacturer did not think it reasonable to charge the full expenditure against costs during the year. He has *deferred* the charges and will write them off gradually.

INTANGIBLES

The last entry in our asset column is *PATENTS AND GOODWILL* (Item 15). If our company were a young one, set up to manufacturer some new patented product, it would probably carry its patents at a substantial figure. In fact, *intangibles* of both old and new companies are often of great but generally unmeasurable worth.

Company practice varies considerably in assigning value to intangibles. Proctor & Gamble, despite the tremendous goodwill that has been built up for *Ivory Soap*, has reduced all of its intangibles to the nominal $1. Some of the big cigarette companies, on the contrary, place a high dollar value on the goodwill their brand names enjoy. Companies that spend a good deal for research and the development of new products are more inclined than others to reflect this fact in the value assigned to patents, license agreements, etc.

LIABILITIES

The liability side of the balance sheet appears a little deceptive at first glance. Several of the entries simply don't sound like liabilities by any ordinary definition of the term.

The first term on the liability side of any balance sheet is usually CURRENT LIABILITIES (Item 16). This is a companion to the Current Assets item across the page and includes all debts that fall due within the next year. The relation between current assets and current liabilities is one of the most revealing things to be gotten from the balance sheet, but we will go into that quite thoroughly later on.

ACCOUNTS PAYABLE (Item 17) represents the money that the company owes to its ordinary business creditors—unpaid bills for materials, supplies, insurance, and the like. Many companies itemize the money they owe in a much more detailed fashion than we have done, but, as you will see, the totals are the most interesting thing to us.

Item 18, ACCRUED TAXES, is the tax bill that the company estimates it still owes for the past year. We have lumped all taxes in our balance sheet, as many companies do. However, sometimes you will find each type of tax given separately. If the detailed procedure is followed, the description of the tax is usually quite sufficient to identify the separate items.

Accounts Payable was defined as the money the company owed to its regular business creditors. The company also owes, on any given day, wages to its own employees; interest to its bondholders and to banks from which it may have borrowed money; fees to its attorneys; pensions, etc. These are all totaled under ACCRUED WAGES, INTEREST AND OTHER EXPENSES (Item 19).

TOTAL CURRENT LIABILITIES (Item 20) is just the sum of everything that the company owed on December 31 and which must be paid sometime in the next twelve months.

It is quite clear that all of the things discussed above are liabilities. The rest of the entries on the liability side of the balance sheet, however, do not seem at first glance to be liabilities.

Our balance sheet shows that the company, on December 31, had $2,000,000 of 3½ percent First Mortgage BONDS outstanding (Item 21). Legally, the money received by a company when it sells bonds is considered a loan to the company. Therefore, it is obvious that the company owes to the bondholders an amount equal to the face value or the *call price* of the bonds it has outstanding. The call price is a figure usually larger than the face value of the bonds at which price the company can *call* the bonds in from the bondholders and pay them off before they ordinarily fall due. The date that often occurs as part of the name of a bond is the date at which the company has promised to pay off the loan from the bondholders.

RESERVES

The next heading, RESERVE FOR CONTINGENCIES (Item 22) sounds more like an asset than a liability. "My reserves," you might say, "are dollars in the bank, and dollars in the bank are assets.

No one would deny that you have something there. In fact, the corporation treasurer also has his reserve for contingencies balanced by either cash or some kind of unspecified investment on the asset side of the ledger. His reason for setting up a reserve on the liability side of the balance sheet is a precaution against making his financial position seem better than it is. He decided that the company might have to pay out this money during the coming year if certain things happened. If he did not set up the "reserve," his surplus would appear larger by an amount equal to his reserve.

A very large reserve for contingencies or a sharp increase in this figure from the previous year should be examined closely by the investor. Often, in the past, companies tried to hide their true earnings by transferring funds into a contingency reserve. As a reserve looks somewhat like a true liability, stockholders were confused about the real value of their securities. When a reserve is not set up for protection against some very probable loss or expenditure, it should be considered by the investor as part of surplus.

CAPITAL STOCK

Below reserves there is a major heading, CAPITAL STOCK (Item 23). Companies may have one type of security outstanding, or they may have a dozen. All of the issues that represent shares of ownership are capital, regardless of what they are called on the balance sheet—preferred stock, preference stock, common stock, founders' shares, capital stock, or something else.

Our typical company has one issue of 5 percent PREFERRED STOCK (Item 24). It is called *preferred* because those who own it have a right to dividends and assets before the *common* stockholders—that is, the holders are in a preferred position as owners. Usually, preferred stockholders do not have a voice in company affairs unless the company fails to pay them dividends at the promised rate. Their rights to dividends are almost always *cumulative*. This simply means that all past dividends must be paid before the other stockholders can receive anything. Preferred stockholders are not creditors of the company so it cannot properly be said that the company *owes* them the value of their holdings. However, in case the company decided to go out of business, preferred stockholders would have a prior claim on anything that was left in the company treasury after all of the creditors, including the bondholders, were paid off. In practice, this right does not always mean much, but it does explain why the book value of their holdings is carried as a liability.

COMMON STOCK (Item 25) is simple enough as far as definition is concerned. It represents the rights of the ordinary owner of the company. Each company has as many owners as it has stockholders. The proportion of the company that each stockholder owns is determined by the number of shares he has. However, neither the book value of a no-par common stock, nor the par value of an issue that has a given par, can be considered as representing either the original sale price, the market value, or what would be left for the stockholders if the company were liquidated.

A profitable company will seldom be dissolved. Once things have taken such a turn that dissolution appears desirable, the stated value of the stock is generally nothing but a fiction. Even if the company is profitable as a going institution, once it ceases to function even its tangible assets drop in value because there is not usually a ready market for its inventory of raw materials and semi-finished goods, or its plant and machinery.

SURPLUS

The last major heading on the liability side of the balance sheet is SURPLUS (Item 26). The surplus, of course, is not a liability in the popular sense at all. It represents, on our balance sheet, the difference between the stated value of our common stock and the net assets behind the stock.

Two different kinds of surplus frequently appear on company balance sheets, and our company has both kinds. The first type listed is *EARNED* surplus (Item 27). Earned surplus is roughly similar to your own savings. To the corporation, earned surplus is that part of net income which has not been paid to stockholders as dividends. It still belongs to you, but the directors have decided that it is best for the company and the stockholders to keep it in the business. The surplus may be invested in the plant just as you might invest part of your savings in your home. It may also be in cash or securities.

In addition to the earned surplus, our company also has a CAPITAL surplus (Item 28) of $1,900.00, which the balance sheet explains arose from selling the stock at a higher cost per share than is given as its stated value. A little arithmetic shows that the stock is carried on the books at $2.50 a share while the capital surplus amounts to $4.75 a share. From this we know that the company actually received an average of $7.25 net a share for the stock when it was sold.

WHAT DOES THE BALANCE SHEET SHOW?

Before we undertake to analyze the balance sheet figures, a word on just what an investor can expect to learn is in order. A generation or more ago, before present accounting standards had gained wide acceptance, considerable imagination went into the preparation of balance sheets. This, naturally, made the public skeptical of financial reports. Today, there is no substantial ground for skepticism. The certified public accountant, the listing requirements of the national stock exchanges, and the regulations of the Securities and Exchange Commission have, for all practical purposes, removed the grounds for doubting the good faith of financial reports.

The investor, however, is still faced with the task of determining the significance of the figures. As we have already seen, a number of items are based, to a large degree, upon estimates, while others are, of necessity, somewhat arbitrary.

NET WORKING CAPITAL

There is one very important thing that we can find from the balance sheet and accept with the full confidence that we know what we are dealing with. That is net working capital, sometimes simply called working capital.

On the asset side of our balance sheet, we have added up all of the current assets and show the total as Item 6. On the liability side, Item 20 gives the total of current liabilities. *Net working capital* or *net current assets* is the difference left after subtracting current liabilities from current assets. If you consider yourself an investor rather than a speculator, you should always insist that any company in which you invest have a comfortable amount of working capital. The ability of a company to meet its obligations with ease, expand its volume as business expands and take advantage of opportunities as they present themselves, is, to an important degree, determined by its working capital.

Probably the question in your mind is: "*Just what does 'comfortable amount' of working capital mean?*" Well, there are several methods used by analysts to judge whether a particular company has a sound working capital position. The first rough test for an industrial company is to compare the working capital figure with the current liability total. Most analysts say that minimum safety requires that net working capital at least equal current liabilities. Or, put another way, current assets should be at least twice as large as current liabilities.

There are so many different kinds of companies, however, that this test requires a great deal of modification if it is to be really helpful in analyzing companies in different industries. To help you interpret the current position of a company in which you are considering investing, the *current ratio* is more helpful than the dollar total of working capital. The current ratio is current assets divided by current liabilities.

In addition to working capital and current ratio, there are two other ways of testing the adequacy of the current position. *Net quick assets* provide a rigorous and important test of a company's ability to meet its current obligations. Net quick assets are found by taking total current assets (Item 6) and subtracting the value of inventories (Item 5). A well-fixed industrial company should show a reasonable excess of quick assets over current liabilities.

Finally, many analysts say that a good industrial company should have at least as much working capital (current assets less current liabilities) as the total book value of its bonds and preferred stock. In other words, current liabilities, bonded debt, and preferred stock *altogether* should not exceed the current assets.

INVENTORY AND INVENTORY TURNOVER

In the recent past, there has been much talk of inventories. Many commentators have said that these carry a serious danger to company earnings if management allows them to increase too much. Of course, this has always been true, but present high prices have made everyone more inventory-conscious than usual.

There are several dangers in a large inventory position. In the first place, sharp drop in price may cause serious losses; also, a large inventory may indicate that the company has accumulated a big supply of unsalable merchandise. The question still remains, however: "What do we mean by large inventory?"

As you certainly realize, an inventory is large or small only in terms of the yearly turnover and the type of business. We can discover the annual turnover of our sample company by dividing inventories (Item 5) into total annual sales (item "a" on the income account).

It is also interesting to compare the value of the inventory of a company being studied with total current assets. Again, however, there is considerable variation between different types of companies, so that the relationship becomes significant only when compared with similar companies.

NET BOOK VALUE OF SECURITIES

There is one other very important thing that can be gotten from the balance sheet, and that is the net book or equity value of the company's securities. We can calculate the net book value of each of the three types of securities our company has outstanding by a little very simple arithmetic. *Book value* means *the value at which something is carried on the books of the company*.

The full rights of the bondholders come before any of the rights of the stockholders, so, to find the net book value or net tangible assets backing up the bonds we add together the balance sheet value of the bonds, preferred stock, common stock, reserve, and surplus. This gives us a total of $9,630,000, (We would not include contingency reserve if we were reasonably sure the contingency was going to arise, but, as general reserves are often equivalent to surplus, it is, usually, best to treat the reserve just as though it were surplus.) However, part of this value represents the goodwill and patents carried at $100,000, which is not a tangible item, so, to be conservative, we subtract this amount, leaving $9,530,000 as the total net book value of the bonds. This is equivalent to $4,765 for each $1,000 bond, a generous figure. To calculate the net book value of the preferred stock, we must eliminate the face value of the bonds, and then, following the same procedure, add the value of the preferred stock, common stock, reserve, and surplus, and subtract goodwill. This gives us a total net book value for the preferred stock of $7,530 or $753 for each share of $100 par value preferred. This is also very good coverage for the preferred stock, but we must examine current earnings before becoming too enthusiastic about the value of any security.

The net book value of the common stock, while an interesting figure, is not so important as the coverage on the senior securities. In case of liquidation, there is seldom much left for the common stockholders because of the normal loss in value of company assets when they are put up for sale, as mentioned before. The book value figure, however, does give us a basis for comparison with other companies. Comparisons of net book value over a period of years also show us if the company is a soundly growing one or, on the other hand, is losing ground. Earnings, however, are our important measure of common stock values, as we will see shortly.

The net book value of the common stock is found by adding the stated value of the common stock, reserves, and surplus and then subtracting patents and goodwill. This gives us a total net book value of $6,530,000. As there are 400,000 shares of common outstanding, each share has a net book value of $16.32. You must be careful not to be misled by book value figures, particularly of common stock. Profitable companies (Coca-Cola, for example) often show a very low net book value and very substantial earnings. Railroads, on the other hand, may show a high book value for their common stock but have such low or irregular earnings that the market price of the stock is much less than its apparent book value. Banks, insurance companies, and investment trusts are exceptions to what we have said about common stock net book value. As their assets are largely liquid (i.e., cash, accounts receivable, and marketable securities), the book value of their common stock sometimes indicates its value very accurately.

PROPORTION OF BONDS, PREFERRED AND COMMON STOCK

Before investing, you will want to know the proportion of each kind of security issued by the company you are considering. A high proportion of bonds reduces the attractiveness of both the preferred and common stock, while too large an amount of preferred detracts from the value of the common.

The *bond ratio* is found by dividing the face value of the bonds (Item 21), or $2,000,000, by the total value of the bonds, preferred stock, common stock, reserve, and surplus, or $9,630,000. This shows that bonds amount to about 20 percent of the total of bonds, capital, and surplus.

The *preferred stock ratio* is found in the same way, only we divide the stated value of the preferred stock by the total of the other five items. Since we have half as much preferred stock as we have bonds, the preferred ratio is roughly 10.

Naturally, the *common stock ratio* will be the difference between 100 percent and the totals of the bonds and preferred, or 70 percent in our sample company. You will want to remember that the most valuable method of determining the common stock ratio is in combination with reserve and surplus. The surplus, as we have noted, is additional backing for the common stock and usually represents either original funds paid in to the company in excess of the stated value of the common stock (capital surplus), or undistributed earnings (earned surplus).

Most investment analysts carefully examine industrial companies that have more than about a quarter of their capitalization represented by bonds, while common stock should total at least as much as all senior securities (bonds and preferred issues). When this is not the case, companies often find it difficult to raise new capital. Banks don't like to lend them money because of the already large debt, and it is sometimes difficult to sell common stock because of all the bond interest or preferred dividends that must be paid before anything is available for the common stockholder.

Railroads and public utility companies are exceptions to most of the rules of thumb that we use in discussing The ABC Manufacturing Company, Inc. Their situation is different because of the tremendous amounts of money they have invested in their fixed assets, their small inventories and he ease with which they can collect their receivables. Senior securities of railroads and utility companies frequently amount to more than half of their capitalization, Speculators often interest themselves in companies that have a high proportion of debt or preferred stock because of the *leverage factor*. A simple illustration will show why. Let us take, for example, a company with $10,000,000 of 4 percent bonds outstanding. If the company is earning $440,000 before bond interest, there will be only $40,000 left for the common stock ($10,000,000 at 4% equals $400,000). However, an increase of only 10 percent in earnings (to $484,000) will leave $84,000 for common stock dividends, or an increase of more than 100 percent. If there is only a small common issue, the increase in earnings per share would appear very impressive.

You have probably already noticed that a decline of 10 percent in earnings would not only wipe out everything available for the common stock, but result in the company being unable to cover its full interest on its bonds without dipping into surplus. This is the great danger of so-called high leverage stocks and also illustrates the fundamental weakness of companies that have a disproportionate amount of debt or preferred stock. Investors would do well to steer clear of them. Speculators, however, will continue to be fascinated by the market opportunities they offer.

THE INCOME ACCOUNT

The fundamental soundness of a company, as shown by its balance sheet, is important to investors, but of even greater interest is the record of its operation. Its financial structure shows much of its ability to weather storms and pick up speed when times are good. It is the income record, however, that shows us how a company is actually doing and gives us our best guide to the future.

The *Consolidated Income and Earned Surplus* account of our company is stated on the next page. Follow the items given there and we will find out just how our company earned its money, what it did with its earnings, and what it all means in terms of our three classes of securities. We have used a combined income and surplus account because it is the form most frequently followed by industrial companies. However, sometimes the two statements are given separately. Also, a variety of names are used to describe this same part of the financial report. Sometimes it is called profit and loss account, sometimes *record of earnings*, and, often, simply *income account*. They are all the same thing.

The details that you will find on different income statements also vary a great deal. Some companies show only eight or ten separate items, while others will give a page or more of closely spaced entries that break down each individual type of revenue or cost. We have tried to strike a balance between extremes; give the major items that are in most income statements, omitting details that are only interesting to the expert analyst.

The most important source of revenue always makes up the first item on the income statement. In our company, it is *Net Sales* (Item "a"). If it were a railroad or a utility instead of a manufacturer, this item would be called *gross revenues*. In any case, it represents the money paid into the company by its customers. Net sales are given to show that the figure represents the amount of money actually received after allowing for discounts and returned goods.

Net sales or gross revenues, you will note, is given before any kind of miscellaneous revenue that might have been received from investments, the sale of company property, tax refunds, or the like. A well-prepared income statement is always set up this way so that the stockholder can estimate the success of the company in fulfilling its major job of selling goods or service. If this were not so, you could not tell whether the company was really losing or making money on its operations, particularly over the last few years when tax rebates and other unusual things have often had great influence on final net income figures.

The ABC Manufacturing Company, Inc.
CONSOLIDATED INCOME AND EARNED SURPLUS
For the Year Ended December 31

Item		
a. Sales		$10,000,000
b. COST OF SALES, EXPENSES AND OTHER OPERATING CHARGES:		
c. Cost of Goods Sold	$7,000,000	
d. Selling, Administrative & Gen. Expenses	500,000	
e. Depreciation	200,000	
f. Maintenance and Repairs	400,000	
g. Taxes (Other than Federal Inc. Taxes)	300,000	8,400,000
h. NET PROFIT FROM OPERATIONS		$1,600,000
i. OTHER INCOME:		
j. Royalties and Dividends	$250,000	
k. Interest	25,000	
l. TOTAL		$1,875,000
m. INTEREST CHARGES:		
n. Interest on Funded Debt	$70,000	
o. Other Interest	20,000	90,000
p. NET INCOME BEFORE PROVISION FOR FED. INCOME TAXES		$1,785,000
q. PROVISION FOR FEDERAL INCOME TAXES		678,300
r. NET INCOME		$1,106,700
s. DIVIDENDS		
t. Preferred Stock - $5.00 Per Share	$50,000	
u. Common Stock - $1.00 Per Share	400,000	
v. PROVISION FOR CONTINGENCIES	200,000	650,000
w. BALANCE CARRIED TO EARNED SURPLUS		456,700
x. EARNED SURPLUS – JANUARY 1		3,073,000
y. EARNED SURPLUS – DECEMBER 31		$3,530,000

COST OF SALES

A general heading, *Cost of Sales, Expenses, and Other Operating Charges* (Item "b") is characteristic of a manufacturing company, but a utility company or railroad would call all of these things *operating expenses*.

The most important subdivision is *Cost of Goods Sold* (Item "c"). Included under cost of goods sold are all of the expenses that go directly into the manufacture of the products the company sells—raw materials, wages, freight, power, and rent. We have lumped these expenses together, as many companies do. Sometimes, however, you will find each item listed separately. Analyzing a detailed income account is a pretty technical operation and had best be left to the expert.

We have shown separately, opposite "d," the *Selling, Administrative and General Expenses* of the past year. Unfortunately, there is little uniformity among companies in their treatment of these important non-manufacturing costs. Our figure includes the expenses of management; that is, executive salaries and clerical costs; commissions and salaries paid to salesmen; advertising expenses, and the like.

Depreciation ("e") shows us the amount that the company transferred from income during the year to the depreciation reserve that we ran across before as Item "11" on the balance sheet (Page 2). Depreciation must be charged against income unless the company is going to live on its own fat, something that no company can do for long and stay out of bankruptcy.

MAINTENANCE

Maintenance and Repairs (Item "f") represents the money spent to keep the plant in good operating order. For example, the truck that we mentioned under depreciation must be kept running day by day. The cost of new tires, recharging the battery, painting and mechanical repairs are all maintenance costs. Despite this day-to-day work on the truck, the company must still provide for the time when it wears out—hence, the reserve for depreciation.

You can readily understand from your own experience the close connection between maintenance and depreciation. If you do not take good care of your own car, you will have to buy a new one sooner than you would had you maintained it well. Corporations face the same problem with all of their equipment. If they do not do a good job of maintenance, much more will have to be set aside for depreciation to replace the abused tools and property.

Taxes are always with us. A profitable company always pays at least two types of taxes. One group of taxes are paid without regard to profits, and include real estate taxes, excise taxes, social security, and the like (Item "g"). As these payments are a direct part of the cost of doing business, they must be included before we can determine the *Net Profit From Operations* (Item "h").

Net Profit From Operations (sometimes called *gross profit*) tells us what the company made from manufacturing and selling its products. It is an interesting figure to investors because it indicates how efficiently and successfully the company operates in its primary purpose as a creator of wealth. As a glance at the income account will tell you, there are still several other items to be deducted before the stockholder can hope to get anything. You can also easily imagine that for many companies these other items may spell the difference between profit and loss. For these reasons, we use net profit from operations as an indicator of progress in manufacturing and merchandising efficiency, not as a judge of the investment quality of securities.

Miscellaneous Income not connected with the major purpose of the company is generally listed after net profit from operations. There are quite a number of ways that corporations increase their income, including interest and dividends on securities they own, fees for special services performed, royalties on patents they allow others to use, and tax refunds. Our income statement shows *Other Income* as Item "i," under which is shown income from *Royalties* and *Dividends* (Item "j"), and as a separate entry, *Interest* (Item "k") which the company received from its bond investments. The *Total* of other income (Item "l") shows us how much The ABC Manufacturing Company received from so-called *outside activities*. Corporations with diversified interests often receive tremendous amounts of other income.

INTEREST CHARGES

There is one other class of expenses that must be deducted from our income before we can determine the base on which taxes are paid, and that is *Interest Charges* (Item "m"). As our company has $2,000,000 worth of 3 ½ percent bonds outstanding, it will pay *Interest on Funded Debt* of $70,000 (Item "n"). During the year, the company also borrowed money from the bank, on which it, of course, paid interest, shown as *Other Interest* (Item "o").

Net Income Before Provision for Federal Income Taxes ("Item "p") is an interesting figure for historical comparison. It shows us how profitable the company was in all of its various operations. A comparison of this entry over a period of years will enable you to see how well the company had been doing as a business institution before the government stepped in for its share of net earnings. Federal taxes have varied so much in recent years that earnings before taxes are often a real help in judging business progress.

A few paragraphs back we mentioned that a profitable corporation pays two general types of taxes. We have already discussed those that are paid without reference to profits. *Provision for Federal Income Taxes* (Item "q") is ordinarily figured on the total income of the company after normal business expenses, and so appears on our income account below these charges. Bond interest, for example, as it is payment on a loan, is deducted beforehand. Preferred and common stock dividends, which are profits that go to owners of the company, come after all charges and taxes.

NET INCOME

After we have deducted all of our expenses and income taxes from total income, we get *Net Income* (Item "r"). Net income is the most interesting figure of all to the investor. Net income is the amount available to pay dividends on the preferred and common stock. From the balance sheet, we have learned a good deal about the company's stability and soundness of structure; from net profit from operations, we judge whether the company is improving in industrial efficiency. Net income tells us whether the securities of the company are likely to be a profitable investment.

The figure given for a single year is not nearly all of the store, however. As we have noted before, the historical record is usually more important than the figure for any given year. This is just as true of net income as any other item. So many things change from year to year that care must be taken not to draw hasty conclusions. During the war, Excess Profits Taxes had a tremendous effect on the earnings of many companies. In the next few years, carryback tax credits allowed some companies to show a net profit despite the fact that they had operated at a loss. Even net income can be a misleading figure unless one examines it carefully. A rough and easy way of judging how sound a figure it is would be to compare it with previous years.

The investor in stocks has a vital interest in *Dividends* (Item "s"). The first dividend that our company must pay is that on its *Preferred Stock* (Item "t"). Some companies will even pay preferred dividends out of earned surplus accumulated in the past if the net income is not large enough, but such a company is skating on thin ice unless the situation is most unusual.

The directors of our company decided to pay dividends totaling ($400,000 on the *Common Stock*, or $1 a share (Item "u"). As we have noted before, the amount of dividends paid is not determined by net income, but by a decision of the stockholders' representatives—the company's directors. Common dividends, just like preferred dividends, can be paid out of surplus if there is little or no net income. Sometimes companies do this if they have a long history of regular payments and don't want to spoil the record because of some special temporary situation that caused them to lose money. This occurs even less frequently and is more dangerous than paying preferred dividends out of surplus.

It is much more common, on the contrary, to plough earnings back into the business—a phrase you frequently see on the financial pages and in company reports. The directors of our typical company have decided to pay only $1 on the common stock, though net income would have permitted them to pay much more. They decided that the company should save the difference.

The next entry on our income account, *Provision for Contingencies* (Item "v") shows us where our reserve for contingencies arose. The treasurer of our typical company has put the provision for contingencies after dividends. However, you will discover, if you look at very many financial reports, that it is sometimes placed above net income.

All of the net income that was not paid out as dividends, or set aside for contingencies, is shown as *Balance Carried to Earned Surplus* (Item "w"). In other words, it is kept in the business. In previous years, the company had also earned more than it paid out so it had already accumulated by the beginning of the year an earned surplus of $3,073,000 (Item "x"). When we total the earned surplus accumulated during the year to that which the company had at the first of the year, we get the total earned surplus at the end of the year (Item "y"). You will notice that the total here is the same as that which we ran across on the balance sheet as Item 27.

Not all companies combine their income and surplus account. When they do not, you will find that *balance carried to surplus* will be the last item on the income account. The statement of consolidated surplus would appear as a third section of the corporation's financial report. A separate surplus account might be used if the company shifted funds for reserves to surplus during the year or made any other major changes in its method of treating the surplus account.

ANALYZING THE INCOME ACCOUNT

The income account, like the balance sheet, will tell us a lot more if we make a few detailed comparisons. The size of the totals on an income account doesn't mean much by itself. A company can have hundreds of millions of dollars in net sales and be a very bad investment. On the other hand, even a very modest profit in round figure may make a security attractive if there are only a small number of shares outstanding.

Before you select a company for investment, you will want to know something of its *margin of profit*, and how this figure has changed over the years. Finding the margin of profit is very simple. We just divide the net profit from operations (Item "h") by net sales (Item "a"). The figure we get (0.16) shows us that the company made a profit of 16 percent from operations. By itself, though, this is not very helpful. We can make it significant in two ways.

In the first place, we can compare it with the margin of profit in previous years, and, from this comparison, learn if the company excels other companies that do a similar type of business. If the margin of profit of our company is very low in comparison with other companies in the same field, it is an unhealthy sign. Naturally, if it is high, we have grounds to be optimistic.

Analysts also frequently use *operating ratio* for the same purpose. The operating ratio is the complement of the margin of profit. The margin of profit of our typical company is 16. The operating ratio is 84. You can find the operating ratio either by subtracting the margin of profit from 100 or dividing the total of operating costs ($8,400,000) by net sales ($10,000,000).

The margin of profit figure and the operating ratio, like all of those ratios we examined in connection with the balance sheet, give us general information about the company, help us judge its prospects for the future. All of these comparisons have significance for the long term as they tell us about the fundamental economic condition of the company. But you still have the right to ask: "Are the securities good investments for me now?"

Investors, as opposed to speculators, are primarily interested in two things. The first is safety for their capital and the second, regularity of income. They are also interested in the rate of return on their investment but, as you will see, the rate of return will be affected by the importance placed on safety and regularity. High income implies risk. Safety must be bought by accepting a lower return.

The safety of any security is determined primarily by the earnings of the company that are available to pay interest or dividends on the particular issues. Again, though, round dollar figures aren't of much help to us. What we want to know is the relationship between the total money available and the requirements for each of the securities issued by the company.

INTEREST COVERAGE

As the bonds of our company represent part of its debt, the first thing we want to know is how easily the company can pay the interest. From the income account we see that the company had total income of $1,875,000 (Item "1"). The interest charge on our bonds each year is $70,000 (3½ percent of $2,000,000—Item 21 on the balance sheet). Dividing total income by bond interest charges ($1,875,000 by $70,000) shows us that the company earned its bond interest 26 times over. Even after income taxes, bond interest was earned 17 times, a method of testing employed by conservative analysts. Before an industrial bond should be considered a safe investment, so our company has a wide margin of safety.

To calculate the *preferred dividend coverage* (i.e., the number of times preferred dividends were earned), we must use net income as our base, as Federal Income Taxes and all interest charges must be paid before anything is available for stockholders. As we have 10,000 shares of $100 par value of preferred stock which pays a dividend of 5 percent, the total dividend requirement for the preferred stock is $50,000 (Items 24 on the balance sheet and "t" on the income account).

EARNINGS PER COMMON SHARE

The buyer of common stocks is often more concerned with the earnings per share of his stock than he is with the dividend. It is usually earnings per share or, rather, prospective earnings per share, that influence stock market prices. Our income account does not show the earnings available for the common stock, so we must calculate it ourselves. It is net income less preferred dividends (Items "r"- "t"), or $1,056,700. From the balance sheet, we know that there are 400,000 shares outstanding, so the company earned about $2.64 per share.

All of these ratios have been calculated for a single year. It cannot be emphasized too strongly, however, that the record is more important to the investor than the report of any single year. By all the tests we have employed, both the bonds and the preferred stock of our typical company appear to be very good investments, if their market prices were not too high. The investor would want to look back, however, to determine whether the operations were reasonably typical of the company.

Bonds and preferred stocks that are very safe usually sell at pretty high prices, so the yield to the investor is small. For example, if our company has been showing about the same coverage on its preferred dividends for many years and there is good reason to believe that the future will be equally kind, the company would probably replace the old 5 percent preferred with a new issue paying a lower rate, perhaps 4 percent.

STOCK PRICES

As the common stock does not receive a guaranteed dividend, its market value is determined by a great variety of influences in addition to the present yield of the stock measured by its dividends. The stock market, by bringing together buyers and sellers from all over the world, reflects their composite judgment of the present and future value of the stock. We cannot attempt here to write a treatise on the stock market. There is one important ratio, however, that every common stock buyer considers. That is the ratio of earnings to market price.

The so-called *price-earnings ratio* is simply the earnings per share on the common stock divided into the market price. Our typical company earned $2.64 a common share in the year. If the stock were selling at $30 a share, its price-earnings ratio would be about 11.4. This is the basis figure that you would want to use in comparing the common stock of this particular company with other similar stocks.

17

IMPORTANT TERMS AND CONCEPTS

LIABILITIES
    WHAT THE COMPANY OWES—+ RESERVES + SURPLUS + STOCKHOLDERS INTEREST IN THE COMPANY

ASSETS
    WHAT THE COMPANY OWNS— + WHAT IS OWED TO THE COMPANY

FIXED ASSETS
    MACHINERY, EQUIPMENT, BUILDINGS, ETC.

EXAMPLES OF FIXED ASSETS
    DESKS, TABLES, FILING CABINETS, BUILDINGS, LAND, TIMBERLAND, CARS AND TRUCKS, LOCOMOTIVES AND FREIGHT CARS, SHIPYARDS, OIL LANDS, ORE DEPOSITS, FOUNDRIES

EXAMPLES OF:
    PREPAID EXPENSES
        PREPAID INSURANCE, PREPAID RENT, PREPAIDD ROYALTIES AND PREPAID INTEREST

    DEFERRED CHARGES
        AMORTIZATION OF BOND DISCOUNT, ORGANIZATION EXPENSE, MOVING EXPENSES, DEVELOPMENT EXPENSES

ACCOUNTS PAYABLE
    BILLS THE COMPANY OWES TO OTHERS

BONDHOLDERS ARE CREDITORS
    BOND CERTIFICATES ARE IOU'S ISSUED BY A COMPANY BACKED BY A PLEDGE

BONDHOLDERS ARE OWNERS
    A STOCK CERTIFICATE IS EVIDENCE OF THE SHAREHOLDER'S OWNERSHIP

EARNED SURPLUS
    INCOME PLOWED BACK INTO THE BUSINESS

NET SALES
    GROSS SALES MINUS DISCOUNTS AND RETURNED GOODS

NET INCOME
    = TOTAL INCOME MINUS ALL EXPENSES AND INCOME TAXES

www.ingramcontent.com/pod-product-compliance
Lightning Source LLC
Chambersburg PA
CBHW081823300426
44116CB00014B/2460